Memories of Dunoon & Cowal is the much asked for new edition of Renée Forsyth's popular and acclaimed account of all aspects of Dunoon and the Cowal Peninsula.

From the ancient and bloody conflict between the Campbells and the Lamonts to the rise of Dunoon as a 'doon the watter' visitor venue in the nineteenth century. From the influence of visitors on villages like Kirn, Innellan and Kilmun to the arrival of the US Navy in the Holy Loch in the 1960s. And local institutions like the world famous Cowal Highland Gathering. No memory is left unexplored.

Characters from 'Highland Mary' Campbell, the love of Robert Burns, to marine engineer David Napier of Kilmun, from music hall supremo Harry Lauder to author Neil Munro, as well as some worthies of more recent memory – all are covered in their connections with Cowal.

Thoroughly researched and crammed with treasured detail, this new edition contains many original photos.

Renée Forsyth was born in Berlin. After her family left Germany in 1935, she was educated in England and Switzerland. She had a successful career in advertising and publishing before becoming a freelance writer and editorial consultant.

Memories

of

Dunoon & Cowal

Renée Forsyth

Argyll
publishing

© Renée Forsyth 1997
Argyll Publishing
Glendaruel
Argyll PA22 3AE
www.argyllpublishing.com

First edition 1983 Argyll Reproductions
This edition first printing 1997
Second printing 2005

British Library Cataloguing in Publication Data.
A catalogue record for this book is available from
the British Library.

ISBN 1874640 43 2

Origination
Cordfall Ltd, Glasgow

Printing
Cromwell Press

God gives all men all earth to love,
But, since man's heart is small,
Ordains for each one spot shall prove
Belovèd over all.

Rudyard Kipling

Contents

Acknowledgements

I SHOULD like to express my heartfelt thanks to everyone in the local community who gave me so much help during the writing of this book. Without them and the editors of newspapers, magazines and periodicals throughout Britain, Ireland and the Commonwealth, who so kindly printed my letter requesting reminiscences about Dunoon, there would have been no book.

My thanks also to Gregor Roy, whose enthusiasm and encouragement kept me buoyant when spirits were flagging, and to Fiona Roy who showed her usual patience when dealing with my many literary queries.

For supplying the many photographs, only a small sample of which we could find space for, and for granting permission to reproduce them I should like to thank the following:

T & R Annan & Son; Argyll & Bute Council Library & Information Service; Argyll, the Isles, Loch Lomond, Stirling & Trossachs Tourist Board (acknowledged in captions as AILLST TB); Duncan Barclay; James Boyd; Stewart Bryson; Cowal Highland Gathering Ltd; Dunoon & Cowal Heritage Society; Dunoon Grammar School; Dunoon Observer & Argyllshire Standard; Hafton Holiday Lodges Ltd; Eileen Lea; Luis Llovet; Molly McLachlan; Mitchell Library; Ordnance Survey; Royal Commission on the Ancient & Historical Monuments of Scotland (RCAHMS); John Saidler; Sandbank Community Council; Younger Botanic Garden, Benmore.

Preface

I expect that many of you picking up this book will be wondering how an 'incomer' has the nerve to write about their beloved corner of the world. The reason is quite simple. I fell in love with Dunoon the first moment I set eyes on it some twenty years ago. My love affair with the area was cemented when my husband and I walked along the shore road to Sandbank past the sylvan grounds of Hafton Estate. Not even the sinister aspect of the Polaris Submarine base could mar the exquisite beauty of the Holy Loch with its breathtaking backcloth of gentle sloping hills. The ever changing light made the place magical and it has seemed so to me ever since.

I feel very lucky indeed to be living in such a beautiful part of the world and hope to make 'old bones' here.

This book is dedicated to all those, past and present, connected with Dunoon and its environs. In particular I should like to thank the kind people from all over the world who responded so generously to my plea for reminiscences of this area. I hope this book will bring back some very happy memories.

Renée Forsyth
January 1997

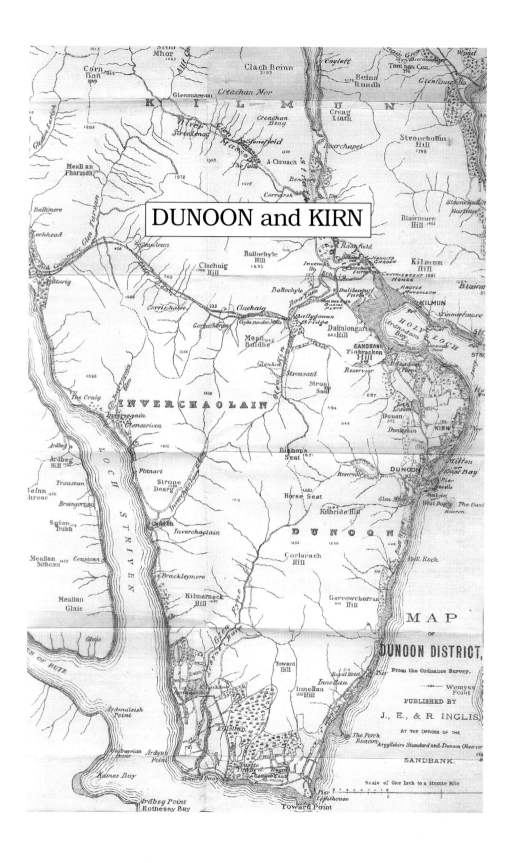

DUNOON and KIRN

MAP

OF

DUNOON DISTRICT,

From the Ordnance Survey.

Wemyss Point

PUBLISHED BY

J., E., & R. INGLIS

AT THE OFFICES OF THE

Argyllshire Standard and Dunoon Observer

SANDBANK.

Scale of One Inch to a Statute Mile

Dunoon Grammar School

**An artist's impression of old Dunoon
showing the Poor House and the Fever
Hospital**

1

The Distant Past

A GREAT NUMBER of small towns exist in Scotland with little or no history attached to them. This cannot be said of Dunoon, one of the most ancient parishes in the country, which dates back to prehistoric times. A cromlech, supposed to be the remains of a Druidical altar, can be seen at Ardnadam Farm, Sandbank. The farm is now a Riding Centre and has a shop, so access to this prehistoric structure is easy. There is also said to be the remains of a Roman camp site on the Ardenslate Golf Course at Kirn.

The origin of the name Dunoon is uncertain, though the claim that it might mean 'the new fort or castle' – *Dun-nuadh* – seems a plausible one, for there was an existing old fort on Dumbarton Rock before the new castle was built at Dunoon.

Dunoon Castle, with its marvellous vantage point over the whole of the Firth of Clyde, must have had great strategic importance in the area as there was plenty of warning of an impending sea attack. Apart from the castle, Dunoon had another advantage. As it was situated on the point nearest the Lowland shores, it was a natural site for a ferry in the days when communication by sea was not only vitally important but much quicker than by land.

On arrival at Dunoon the first sight to greet one is Castle House on the hill. Below it is a huge green mound on which a flag staff can be seen. This is where remain the traces of the ancient castle, and it is thought that at one time the mound was surrounded by the sea.

From the mound one can have a panoramic view of the Clyde, and on a clear day see the dim rock of Ailsa Craig away to the south of the Isle of Arran.

It is believed that a castle existed at Dunoon as early as the eleventh century, and before then it is possible that the Dalriadic Chiefs had a fortress there in 503AD when they first came to settle in Cowal.

Dunoon Castle became one of the original seats of the Lord High Stewards of Scotland and was consequently of great interest and importance to the area. In the twelfth century the castle belonged to the Clan Lamont. Walter Fitz Alan, High Steward of Scotland, had been sent for by King William the Lion to throw out Somerled, Lord of the Isles, who had captured Dunoon Castle. Walter succeeded and then married the heiress of the Lamont Clan. Consequently, part of the Lamont lands in Cowal passed into Stewart hands, descendants of the Steward.

Dunoon Castle, as well as Rothesay Castle, was seized by Sir Edward Balliol in 1333. King Edward III supported a band of disinherited Scottish landowners led by Balliol, and with English help they won several victories including the capture of Dunoon Castle. Edward Balliol was crowned King of Scots, but only at the price of giving away a large part of the Lowlands to the English King. This discredited him in the eyes of his fellow countrymen and the war ended in 1341 with the complete expulsion of the English.

A year later, Robert the Steward, who afterwards became Robert II of Scotland, and Dougall Campbell of Lochawe, landed in Cowal with their galleys and besieged and stormed the castle. From then on it became a royal palace and in 1460 the Lordship of Cowal and the castle of Dunoon were annexed to the patrimony of the Prince of Scotland, and James III granted to Colin, Earl of Argyll, the heritable keepership of the castle with the power of making constables and other officers, thus establishing a strong Campbell foothold in Cowal.

The Earl of Lennox who had hoped to become Regent in Scotland and had worked for the abdication of Mary, Queen of Scots, after the murder of Darnley, in 1544 armed with Henry VIII's authority, appeared in the Firth of Clyde with eighteen ships and six hundred men. He captured Rothesay Castle, tried to seize the castle at Dumbarton, but failed, and then sailed westwards in the hope of capturing Dunoon Castle. He succeeded and the Earl of Argyll abandoned it.

Lennox's soldiers burned down the village and, not content with that, also burned down the church where the villagers had put their worldly possessions for safety.

Ever since the 1300s when Dunoon Castle belonged to the Lamonts and was known as 'the Capital Castle of the Lordship of Cowal', the Campbells had coveted it.

There were all sorts of feuds and skirmishes and these came to a head in June 1646 when the Campbells besieged Sir James Lamont and his clan at his ancestral home, Toward Castle. On surrendering the castle the Lamonts were killed in a manner which, even in that cruel period of history, was particularly ferocious. The Lamonts had agreed to give up the castle on the condition that they should be unharmed. Notwithstanding this promise the Campbells chained them by the feet and bound their hands behind their backs. They kept two hundred persons prisoner under strict guard for days within the castle whilst they plundered and murdered the residents, regardless of age. The remaining inhabitants of the castle and village, and prisoners, were put in boats and taken to Dunoon. There, at the castle, the Campbells hanged thirty-six of the kinsmen and friends of Sir James Lamont. Then they proceeded to murder the rest of their prisoners, some of whom they buried alive.

In 1685 the 9th Earl of Argyll rebelled against James II, but this rebellion failed, and it was at this time that Atholl's men invaded Cowal and largely demolished Dunoon Castle, after which it was never rebuilt. The Campbells gradually made Inverary Castle their home, although they kept Kilmun as the Argyll burial ground.

In those times, instead of squatters taking over empty places, people pilfered the stones of buildings for their own homes, and slowly and surely the castle disappeared, with only a few stones remaining as a reminder that it had once held a most important position in the times of early Dunoon.

T & R Annan

The Victorians, sitting in perfect
decorum on the beach of Dunoon's West
Bay in the 1890s, do not exude an air of
carefree happiness. This may be because
it was rather a dreich day with no one
making use of the amazing number of
bathing huts. The fact that there are so
many of them indicates the popularity
of Dunoon during the summer season

2

The Intrepid Tourist

STANDING IN Argyll Street on a warm summer's day, visitors and shoppers crowding the busy thoroughfare, it is difficult to envisage Dunoon two hundred years ago. Then it was a small sleepy fishing village consisting of a church, a manse and a few slated and thatched cottages.

The most frequent visitors at that time were the drovers, from the isles and the north, who arrived in Dunoon for the short boat journey across to Cloch Point, and then on to the southern cattle markets.

Robert Reid's family were the first recorded tourists to visit Dunoon. In the summer of 1770, Robert's father decided to rent a thatched farmhouse called Deling. As always Mrs Reid took a large stock of food and enough furniture to ensure the family's comfort.

A sailing barge was hired to make the voyage and the family embarked with their household goods at the Broomielaw. The passage down river was going well until the tide set against them at Dunglass, when progress became very slow. A little below Dumbarton Castle the barge stuck on a sandbank. The Reids had to wait patiently until the tide rose and once afloat they continued their voyage to Dunoon, arriving late at night. Apart from a visiting drover or farmer the family were the only strangers in the village and must have been a source of great excitement to the locals who saw so few new faces.

Cowal shore, at that time, was totally unspoilt and Robert remembered numerous seals swimming happily about in all directions and sunning themselves on the rocks. Cloch Lighthouse had not been built and there was just an old dilapidated thatched cottage occupied by the ferryman, Hugh McEwing, who sold foreign spirits and the best small-still whisky.

People were very poor and many lived from distilling whisky. When heavy taxes were imposed on the spirit, illegal distilling and smuggling became rife.

Usually passengers crossing the Firth would stop at the Ferry

House for a 'wee dram' and it was an unspoken arrangement that the ferryman would also have one. Sometimes, though, he overdid it and had great difficulty in launching his boat – no easy task if the tide had ebbed, leaving it high and dry.

Although the villagers were Gaelic-speaking and unable to understand English, Robert spent many happy days during that summer accompanying them at low water to gather sea-urchins and shellfish at the Gantocks.

Robert Reid returned to Dunoon in 1851 when it was an established and flourishing holiday resort. He could not recognise the place and had difficulty in recalling the little clachan that he and his family had visited in his youth. He found it hard to believe it was the same Dunoon.

CASTLE HOUSE, DUNOON

Castle House, Dunoon, built by Glasgow Provost and merchant, James Ewing in 1822. The house and gardens were opened to the public in 1893 when the Gilchrist family, wealthy shipbuilders, sold them to Dunoon Burgh Commissioners. The gardens became the centre of Dunoon's entertainment and it is hard to imagine how busy they were until the advent of 'Package' holidays in the 1950s

James Ewing

18

3

The Passing Years

LITTLE DID James Ewing know when he built his home on Castle Hill in 1822 that Dunoon was to become one of the busiest and most fashionable holiday resorts on the Clyde.

James Ewing, a West India merchant and a Lord Provost of Glasgow, as well as an MP for the city, was not the first wealthy man to build a home on this side of the Firth. He had been pre-empted by James Hunter who, in 1816, had bought Hafton Estate a few miles north of Dunoon. Hunter had commissioned David Hamilton to design a new mansion house in the grounds.

Ewing also used the services of this well-known Scots architect, and David Hamilton, who had designed Castle Toward for Kirkman Finlay, built him a home of considerable grandeur which Ewing modestly called Marine Villa. Later, it was to be renamed, more appropriately, Castle House.

William Campbell bought Castle House from Ewing in 1837, and together with James Hunter of Hafton and A. S. Campbell formed the Castle Company to build steamers for use on the Firth, the first of which was the *Duntr oon Castle*. In 1842 Robert Eglington, a retired Calcutta merchant, became the house's third owner, and the last private inhabitants were the Gilchrist family, wealthy shipbuilders from whom in 1893 Dunoon Burgh Commissioners bought the house and ground for the use of the public.

In later years Councillor Tulloch and his wife each bequeathed £400 to the Town Council for a Public Library which was eventually established on the first floor of Castle House and named after the benefactors. Admission to the reading and recreational rooms at that time cost one penny. The ground floor was used as Council Chambers.

The library no longer exists in Castle House. A new library was built in Argyll Street and opened to the public on 12 March 1993. Inside the new library is the Tulloch Reference Room. In place of the library in Castle House is the Castle House Museum.

Henry Bell (1767 – 1830) the pioneer of steam navigation. Most often associated with Helensburgh, his pioneering work to bring the *Comet* into commericial service, opened up undreamed of possibilities for Clyde settlements such as Dunoon. Within a few years of *Comet*'s first voyage carrying fare-paying passengers in 1812, dozens of other operators were sailing the Clyde

When James Ewing built his house there were sixteen small steamboats plying on the Clyde and passengers were transported to and from them by small ferryboats operating from jetties which had been built by private companies and rented out to the steamer owners. As can be imagined this was often dangerous owing to heavy seas and high winds that frequently assaulted the coast. Accidents sometimes occurred and many a time passengers would have to wait, much to their inconvenience, aboard the ship until the weather had moderated.

In 1835 a quay was built which enabled passengers to step directly on to the shore from the steamer, and this was replaced some ten years later by a new pier. The pier was being built for Hunter of Hafton by the uncle of the writer Robert Louis Stevenson, who helped to work on the project. The Stevenson family were engineers noted for their building of bridges, harbours and lighthouses.

The town owed its increasing prosperity to the influx of wealthy Glasgow businessmen who, following the example of Hunter, Ewing and Finlay, built holiday homes for their families along the shores of the Clyde. But it was not until the development of the paddle steamer, coupled with that of the railway, that Dunoon's future was assured.

Thus Dunoon in the middle of the nineteenth century found itself the centre of a tourist trade unequalled anywhere in Scotland at that time.

In 1868, owing to the town's increasing importance as a coastal resort and to its rapidly expanding population, Dunoon became a Parliamentary Burgh. After sixty-four years as a Burgh the town was granted a licence by Lord Lyon, King of Arms, to use their chosen Ensign Armorial under which was the town's motto, FORWARD. In 1975 its functions were transferred to the then new Argyll and Bute District Council.

Dunoon's first municipal building was erected in the mid 1870s on a site gifted by Mr MacArthur-Moir of Milton. The town still has memories of that well-known local family as many of the streets have names associated with them.

Despite the increasing population in the town, Dunoon in 1871 still had no piped water supply and had to rely on its one thousand wells. Lighting, too, was a problem as the Esplanades of East and West Bay were only illuminated by oil lamps which blew out in windy weather, leaving the streets perilously dark. It was not until the end of the 1880s that the more reliable gas lamps were used.

By the end of the century the Town Council, who had bought the pier in 1896, decided it needed to be improved. The sum of £50,000 was invested (a great deal of money in those days) but as a hundred paddle steamers were calling at the pier daily it was well worth the expenditure.

The West Bay was extremely popular with everyone, despite not having a sandy beach. There were innumerable boating stations where it was possible to hire a boat and row out to the nearby Gantock rocks and fish to one's heart's content. There was also a model boating pond, and it was not only children who enjoyed playing there. Gentlemen of uncertain age, with great seriousness and enthusiasm, would race their model sailing boats for hours on end.

The West Bay also sported a rather smart Bathing Lido which could cater for 850 bathers, and there were covered terraces holding two thousand spectators as well as cafés, shower rooms and sunbathing platforms.

Dunoon has changed a great deal over the years and much of this has been due to the demise of the paddle steamers which made the Clyde one of the busiest waterways in the world. Nowadays, most people are content to cross the Firth in one of the two car-ferry services that ply between Gourock and Dunoon.

Dunoon has all the attractions of an island without the disadvantages. Because the town is on a peninsula it is possible, without crossing the Clyde, to drive the eighty miles to and from Glasgow through some of Scotland's finest mountain scenery.

The wealth that was made by the few in the nineteenth century in tobacco, cotton, shipping and the manufacturing industries is now more equally distributed. The houses that once belonged to one family and their retinue of servants – often more than the members of the household – are now hotels, guest houses or converted flat dwellings.

Dunoon is the 'Gateway to the Western Highlands' and there are still thousands of visitors each year coming to the area from all over the world. For many of them the town is the starting point for a wonderful holiday which provides them with peace and tranquillity in varied, unspoilt and stunningly beautiful countryside.

Apart from Castle House one of the most striking landmarks to greet the visitor on arrival at Dunoon is the bronze statue of Mary Campbell, known as 'Highland Mary' because of her soft Gaelic accent.

Mary, the daughter of a sailor, was born in 1764 on the site of Auchamore Farm at the head of Auchamore Road. Her name became synonymous with that of Robert Burns, the greatest lyric poet Scotland has ever produced. Burns, son of an Alloway farmer, became in later life (he died at the age of thirty-seven) a literary, as well as a social, sensation.

But in the early days Robert was a farmer and then an excise man. He met Mary Campbell when she was a nursemaid in the household of Gavin Hamilton. At that time Jean Armour, Burns's wife, was expecting twins, but this did not prevent the poet, a born romantic and womaniser, from plighting his troth with Mary on the banks of the River Ayr on 14th May 1786. In typical Scottish tradition, the lovers exchanged bibles, over running water. This custom signifies that as long as the stream runs, and the Bible holds true, the love will last. (Mary's betrothal bible still exists, as it was bought by one of her nephews who had emigrated to Canada. Later it was bought from him and presented to the trustees of the Burns Monument fund in 1841.)

At that time Burns was hoping to emigrate to Jamaica and Mary had agreed to accompany him as his wife. Mary Campbell left the poet to spend the summer with her family in Campbeltown, where her brother was seriously ill. She nursed him for a while and left for Dunoon. But when she reached Greenock she succumbed to the dreaded fever and died, aged twenty-two, in October 1786, at a house in Minchollop Close.

When Mary died Burns commemorated her with poems like *The Highland Lassie, Will You Go To The Indies, My Mary?, Highland Mary* and his most poignant poem *To Mary in Heaven*.

Mary Campbell was buried in the Old West Church Burying Ground in Greenock where, by public subscription, a gravestone was erected and consecrated in 1842, fifty-six years after her death in the town. There is also a memorial to her at Failford just south of Lochlea, for it was there that the lovers parted forever after their simple exchange of vows.

It was in 1896, on 21st July, the hundredth anniversary of Burns's death, that the ten-and-a-half foot statue was unveiled at Dunoon by Lord and Lady Kelvin. The statue had been sculpted by Ratho-born Watson Stevenson (1842-1904) who was responsible for the Burns statue in Leith, as well as other major works including parts of the Prince Albert Memorial in Stirling, and the poet Tannahill's statue in Paisley. In 1897 railings were put around Mary Campbell's statue to keep off vandals, and in 1964 she was still the centre of attention as someone had the astounding idea of wanting the statue painted in natural colours!

Dunoon Pier was officially opened in 1898, having been bought from the Hafton Estate by Dunoon Burgh Council for £27,000. Originally it had cost £1500 to build! The pier was eventually enlarged so that two steamers could berth simultaneously. Waiting rooms, a goods shed and a signalling tower were added later. In 1934 the pier was the first to install a loudspeaker system, used until the 1970s, to enable the steamer captains to know which berth to use. In 1954 Dunoon had the first major car ferry landing and loading ramp in Scotland

23

ARGYLL STREET, DUNOON.

A busy day in Argyll Street, Dunoon in the early 1900s. It is obvious that there is not much vehicular traffic as people are walking unconcernedly in the middle of the road.
As can be seen the gas lamps first installed in the 1880s are still in use

An Argyll Street scene from the early 1900s. The Post Office remained at the corner of Argyll Street and John Street until 1994 when it moved into the Co-op supermarket in Queen Street

Dunoon & Cowal Heritage Society

A quiet day in Victorian Argyll Street, Dunoon. It would not be long before the horse and carriage would be replaced by the motor car

25

Kirn Pier, with its splendid fine red brick
buildings, was built in 1845. The horses
and carriages awaiting their passengers
here, and at Dunoon, were the
forerunners of the busy taxi trade of
today. The last call at the pier was made
by MV *Cowal* in 1954. Today the pier no
longer exists

4

Kirn

IT IS INTERESTING that people who spent their holiday in Kirn would return year after year. In the past, holiday-makers remained amazingly loyal to their favourite resort and seldom stayed anywhere else.

Kirn, just north of Dunoon and really an extension of it, used to be a thriving little town with its own pier where the paddle steamers used to call throughout the day. In all likelihood the town's name came from a circular quarry behind Ardenslate road. In the process of excavation it got deepened until the quarry had the appearance of a carn – heap of stones.

One of the dominating features on the shore road is the church, a red stone reproduction of early Scottish work with a Celtic-style tall tower. On the foreshore, between Kirn and Hunter's Quay, is an interesting painted, shaped stone nicknamed 'Jim Crow'. Nobody really knows the origin of its name though some think it was called after the son of one of the families who owned a house in the vicinity.

Before and during World War II Nessie Gibson came every summer from Glasgow to spend a month at Kirn, where her mother used to 'take a house'. She remembered becoming acquainted with Miss Aitken who owned a small haberdashery shop on the front. "The unique thing about her was that each day in her back shop Bessie, her housekeeper-companion, prepared a shopping basket full of cubes of bread. Each day at precisely one o'clock Miss Aitken closed her shop and proceeded along the walkways at the front of Kirn sprinkling the bread on the grass for the flock of pigeons which congregated on the roofs of the buildings along the shore road. These pigeons seemed to be 'clock watchers' as, at the stroke of one o' clock, they would swoop down on the grass waiting for Miss Aitken to come along with her basket of bread. This ritual seemed to give her great pleasure, as I am sure it did the pigeons, and she never missed a single day.

"I used to follow her and through time went with her to help distribute her titbits. She was such a kindly soul and let me help her in the shop. To a young girl coming from the concrete jungle of Glasgow this was indeed a treat."

Another happy childhood spent in Kirn was Nan Brown's, who recalled her holiday playmates who asked her and her two younger brothers if they would like to come to 'Aunt Nelly's' with them. "I remember thinking," Nan said, "that Aunt Nelly must be wonderful to welcome any Tom, Dick or Harry to her home. It was only when we arrived at 'Nelly's' that we discovered the real identity of the lady as Antonelli's, the ice-cream parlour."

Nan also had vivid memories of Mr Lorimer whom she considered to be the best boat-hirer in Kirn. "He wore a burnt, deep-sea navy jersey and denim trousers which had been blue at one time but were bleached almost white with sea air, water and sun. He always had a stubby pipe, sometimes upside-down, clenched between his teeth which I never remember him removing from his mouth."

Connie MacFadyn's mother, Elizabeth King, belonged to Dunoon, and her father and three brothers, Charlie, Willie and Tommy, were all cobblers. Connie recalled, "Tommy, who was a bachelor till late in life, had a shop in Kirn facing the pier. He made Harry Lauder's boots. He had his notice up saying 'The King Mends Your Shoes'." Tommy was also remembered by Flora Weir. "Tommy was one of the fast-disappearing local characters. His shop was fronted by a tiny lawn and a flowering bush. One of his many artistic signs read 'All repairs done by the King himself'. The lawn was his pride and joy where he held court in the summer, properly enthroned on a deckchair, while the shoes piled up inside. We were invited to look for our own pairs from amongst the chaos and we always found them."

5
'Doon the Watter'

YOU HAVE ONLY to mention the magic words 'Paddle Steamers' to men and women of a certain age and their eyes will sparkle and glint with unconcealed pleasure. Then a far-away look comes on their faces as they recall those marvellous days when the Clyde was alive with colour and excitement and steamers called regularly throughout the day at the piers that lined the shores of the Firth.

The paddle steamers and their beguiling names – *Jeanie Deans, Guinevere, Red Gauntlet* and *Windsor Castle*, to name just a few – have become the folklore of the Scots, and in the days when they plied the Clyde, were an important part of daily life in the West of Scotland. Old and young alike would be able to identify the steamers miles away by their colours and funnels and argue with absolute certainty that it was indeed the *Dandie Dinmont* and not the *Lucy Ashton* that was racing towards Dunoon.

Those of us lucky enough to have sailed on the *Waverley,* the last of the paddlers on the Clyde, will know a little of the bewitching quality that these ships had for the millions of people who sailed on them. One has only to see the enormous crank-shafts of the engine rotating the great paddle-wheels and to feel the urgent power through the soles of one's feet, to share something of the excitement that accompanied a passage on the old paddle steamers. The *Waverley* was donated to the Paddle Steamer Preservation Society in 1973. She is now as popular on the Thames, Solent and Bristol Channel as she is on the Clyde. Since she began sailing again under the flag of the Waverley Steam Navigation Company in 1975 she has carried more than four million passengers.

Long before the day of the paddle steamer, sailing barges, called wherries, operated at strategic points between opposite sides of the lochs and between island and mainland, from where travellers were picked up. The wherries not only carried passengers, but often cattle and other livestock.

Lord Dundas, a Governor of the Forth and Clyde Canal,

commissioned the world's first steam-propelled vessel the *Charlotte Dundas*. Named after his daughter, she was built on the Clyde and made her maiden voyage in 1802, covering a distance of twenty miles. All this was three years before Nelson's victory at Trafalgar.

In 1807 the American, Robert Fulton, launched a steamship on the Hudson River, and it is certain that he received a great deal of help in its construction from Scots born Henry Bell, whose name is forever linked with the steamers on the Clyde.

Henry Bell was born in 1767 at Torphichen, Linlithgowshire. After going to the village school he was apprenticed to his uncle, a millwright. After qualifying in this trade Bell went to Bo'ness to become a ship-modeller and then worked under John Rennie, the famous engineer, in London. In 1790 he returned to Glasgow, worked as a carpenter, and then moved to Helensburgh on the Clyde coast where he continued his mechanical projects and also worked as an engineer. In 1807 he bought the Baths Hotel which was to become one of the best hotels on the Firth.

Bell had the idea of building a small 42-foot wooden boat to be powered by steam and to have four paddles (later he used only two). He commissioned John Wood of Port Glasgow to build the boat and obtained the services of the famous inventor and blacksmith, David Napier, to construct the boiler and castings. The four-horsepower engine made by John Robertson of Glasgow is part of the Museum of Transport's collection in the city. Henry Bell called the boat the *Comet* after the famous meteor which had been seen in the sky at that time.

On 2nd August 1812 the *Comet* was launched and ran a regular service from Glasgow's Broomielaw to Greenock on alternate days of the week returning on the interim days. Soon the service was extended to the Western Highlands. In 1820 when the *Comet* was returning from Fort William in a severe winter gale she was swept ashore and wrecked.

Although Bell died in November 1830 his inventiveness and effort led to a great expansion in steamboat building. One consequence was the development of the watering places along the shores of the Clyde, and with easier access from Glasgow by steamer, people began to see the future of the Firth's coastline for holidays and seaside homes.

One problem remained, however, and that was to get passengers ashore, for few places had a harbour, let alone a pier, at which the vessels could berth. Passengers, therefore, had to be landed by rowing boat and it was quite usual to deposit them opposite their houses along the Bullwood and Innellan shores.

Early on the steamers were chartered for special purposes and official excursions. In 1835 the *Northern Yacht* was chartered for the annual inspection of lighthouses. The ship was a great favourite with the Glasgow magistrates and it was never discovered whether it was

T & R Annan

**A typical July Fair Saturday crowd at
Glasgow's Central Station**
**For generations, people poured out of
the factories and offices to board trains
to the coast where they connected with
steamers taking them to the Clyde
resorts**
**For most, it was their one chance to get
away from the environment of smoke
and grime where they lived and worked**

EMBARKING AT THE BROOMIELAW, GLASGOW. 5066 G.W.W.

T & R Annan

PS *Chancellor* **at the Broomielaw during the late 1880s. PS** *Vivid* **is lying in the second berth whilst further on is the** *Eagle,* **with** *Guinevere* **paddling slowly down the river. Day trippers went 'doon the watter' to Gourock, Dunoon, Rothesay, Largs and other Clyde resorts**

due to her merits as a boat or to the generous hospitality of the steward on board!

That same year the first wooden jetty was built at Dunoon, and this was followed by other piers along the coast. Until the days of a telegraph between bridge and engine-room the captain used to work his vessel alongside the pier often shouting and swearing, to the offence of the more sensitive passengers.

With the coming of the paddle steamers, Dunoon became a thriving holiday centre for the thousands of ordinary folk working in the dust and grime of smoke-filled Glasgow. Suddenly, people who had never dreamed of being able to have a day out of the city found, that at very little cost, they could have the adventure of an outing on a paddle steamer, embarking at the Broomielaw, to sail down the most glorious waterway in the world, amongst the most breathtaking scenery. The factories, mills and offices seemed a long way away!

From then on going 'Doon the Watter' became a city tradition which lasted for over a century, and the phrase is now part of the language.

The number of steamers which sailed from the Broomielaw down the Clyde was so numerous that at the height of the season the boats would only touch the quay at one point and lay at an angle in the river. Owing to the fierce competition, steamer fares were drastically reduced by the companies in order to win passengers.

L. D. Henderson, grandson of the founder of the famous Clyde Shipyard, Meadowside, writing in 1935, recollected his childhood. "There were at first no railway steamers and no Craigendoran or Gourock piers. The 'star' steamers were the *Columba*, then fairly new and having much shorter funnels than she has had for many years past, and the first *Lord of the Isles*, a Meadowside production.

"Of the morning and evening boats to and from Princes Pier, patronised by the daily travelling commuters of the period, I remember best the *Marquis of Bute* and the *Atholl* which had red funnels with black tops and no saloon accommodation above the main deck, and the *Viceroy* and *Sultana* with white funnels with black tops and half-length saloons. These latter, also built at Meadowside, were precursors of the palatial turbine steamers such as the *King George V* and the *Queen Mary II* and, having been built at Meadowside, were of particular interest to my brother and myself.

"On Saturdays and holidays, when unusually crowded, these narrow cranky vessels, especially the former two, frequently developed alarming lists proceeding for some time with the sponson of one paddlebox completely submerged and then, for apparently no reason, lifting to even keel and, after a moment or two, flopping over to the other side and burying, say, the port paddle-wheel deep in the solid

PS *Duchess of Hamilton*

water while the starboard wheel flapped round like a windmill in the air, which must have made steering almost a fine art."

In 1841 the Glasgow and Greenock railway was opened, and it was this development that gave the real impetus to the future of the paddlers. Other railway companies opened up new lines and at first the steamer companies tried to boycott the railways thinking that because of them their trade would diminish. The reverse happened, and once the railway and steamer companies worked together, business increased considerably. Eventually the railway companies built and owned their own fleets of steamers and gradually incorporated the surviving privately owned companies.

The close of the 1860s saw the real beginning of the diversion of the passenger traffic from Glasgow to the coast, from the direct river steamers to the railway. 'All the way' by boat had lost its charm for the masses. As more and more steamers plied the Clyde competition became fiercer and fiercer and ships could be seen driving full steam ahead, running neck and neck, or rather bow to bow, to make the pier first. Not only was there great excitement among spectators on the shore, but staid business men returning from Glasgow would regularly make bets on the outcome of the race in the same way as punters today back the Grand National or the Derby. Sometimes there were collisions

A paddle steamer leaving Dunoon Pier (1915)

and fines to be paid and, of course, the endless 'post-mortems' on a ship's particular performance.

Soon the railway companies ran their vessels in connection with the trains, and so began the system of 'rail and boat' to and from the coast. There were many companies involved in the steamer traffic but David MacBrayne more or less had the monopoly of the West Highland trade. There is a ditty which goes,

> "The Lord he made the earth
> And over all he reigns,
> Except the West Highland piers
> For they are all MacBraynes."

On Sundays, however, there were no trains owing to Sunday Observance. The pier gates had always been closed on a Sunday and you can imagine the scene when a steamer landed passengers in defiance of the observance. The crowds flocked off the boats, storming the gates. Men did not have too much difficulty in scaling them but it was a different matter for the women, with their long skirts, and the children. Often they would be hurt in the crush. The noise was unbelievable and sometimes there was a near riot.

The disturbances on Sundays became so unpleasant and raucous that in 1896 the town councillors decided that the gates should be opened for the hordes of Glasgow day-trippers. Now that they could get off the pier easily there did not seem to be any problem from the visitors, and local residents had their worst fears allayed.

E.B. Macintyre was on Dunoon pier when the first steamer came in on a Sunday. He remembered the local clergymen telling the townsfolk to stone the trippers for breaking the Sabbath day!

One of the most famous paddle steamers to be launched in 1880, by the Caledonian Steam Packet Company, was the teetotal *Invanhoe* skippered by Captain MacDougall. The Captain wore a gold-braided uniform and his crew dressed like yacht-hands in white blouse with navy blue collar. The *Ivanhoe* was built to avoid the awful drunkenness so frequently to be seen on the other steamers. To everyone's amazement, despite having no alcohol on board, she was an immediate success and sailed on the Clyde for seventeen years.

The *Ivanhoe* was a tremendous favourite with her passengers who were in marked contrast to those who travelled on the other steamers. This may have been because she sailed from Helensburgh and not from Glasgow, only picking up the city passengers when she called at Wemyss Bay. She closely resembled a private yacht in her supreme cleanliness and her white scrubbed deck. She was the first ship to make use of floral decorations on board, and vines, planted in pots and trained across the ceiling in the dining-room, actually produced clusters of grapes. Evening and moonlight cruises were inaugurated and, though these were copied by other steamer companies, only the teetotal *Ivanhoe's* were successful.

In the 1890s the three railway companies, the Caledonian, the North British, and the Glasgow and South Western, along with private companies, such as MacBrayne and Williamson, owned the finest fleet of river steamers in Europe. By the end of the century express trains were leaving hourly to and from Glasgow connecting with steamers for Dunoon, Rothesay and Arran. Dunoon was within three-quarters of an hour's reach of Glasgow – difficult to believe today when the Firth crossing alone takes twenty minutes!

As can be imagined there were many characters among the steamer captains in those days and two of the best known were brothers, Alexander and Thomas (Hamish) McLean.

During their period on the river these two splendid men dispensed more than the average share of practical benevolence. Not withstanding their somewhat gruff manner they let many a poor soul travel free, sometimes with food thrown in.

In those days the dinner in the 'fore cabin' was not the individual table arrangement it was of the steamers' heyday. It had more of the

Mitchell Library

(above) The dining room of the teetotal *Ivanhoe*, built in 1880 and run by the Caledonian Steam Packet Company to avoid the awful drunkenness so frequently seen on other steamers

(below) Before car ferries it was quite usual to have a band on board the steamers. The bands, often German, played all the popular tunes and led singsongs. Here, Charlie Larkin's band entertains an obviously rain-soaked audience

Duncan Barclay

family atmosphere. There was always a chairman who said grace and did the carving, throwing in a good story or two to help digestion.

On one occasion the sea was fairly rough and the cook came down the circular stair with the joint, lost his balance, and the meat fell on the floor. Consternation seized Hamish, but only for a moment. He was equal to the emergency. In a loud voice, so that all could hear him, he ordered the cook to bring down 'the other roast'. This, of course, when it appeared, was the original one wiped down and freshly basted.

A toddy usually completed the meal. In fact, it usually wound up every banquet on board. Tea generally concluded with 'a cinder' in the last cup. On one occasion the cook had made a mistake and instead of filling the tea kettle with water had put in a jug of whisky instead. Everyone was very jolly that evening!

Another story circulated about Hamish. A passenger had complained about the condition of the hand towel he had to use. "A hunner have used it afore ye and ye're the first to complain," retorted Hamish.

Captain Robert Campbell ('Bob' to everyone) of the famous ship-owning family of Kilmun was another well-known and much respected figure on the Clyde. When he died on 10th April 1888 he was buried in Kilmun churchyard. His funeral procession from Glasgow was an extra-ordinary one for a steamboat owner. His coffin was taken to the Broomielaw and put on board *Madge Wildfire*, one of his company's ships. Then she sailed to Kilmun calling at various piers en route. Some of the ships on the river that day flew their flags at half mast, as did many of the shore houses with flag-poles.

One of the favourite holiday jobs for young students was to join the crew of a paddle steamer during the summer months. Many a keen young man could be seen throwing warps to his colleague on shore or securing them to a handy bollard. Some youngsters even became temp-orary pursers, and it may have been one of these students who was on board with a little girl who was visiting her aunt in Dunoon.

Her mother had told her immediately to find the purser when the boat left Glasgow and to ask him to tell her when the boat reached Dunoon. Each time the boat docked at the various piers en route the little girl would approach the purser and ask him if she had arrived. Finally, the purser told her not to keep bothering him and promised that he would let her know when she reached her destination.

However, in the holiday rush he completely forgot all about her until the steamer had left Dunoon pier. He looked up to see the girl watching him with anxious eyes. He dashed up to the bridge, explained the situation to the captain who, furious at the disruption of his time-table, ordered the steamer to return to the pier. The purser, very pleased, went up to the youngster and told her that they were now at

Dunoon. "Thank you," said the little girl sitting down and opening a brown paper bag. "Mummy told me not to eat my sandwiches till we got there."

The interiors of the steamers, with superb furnishings and lovely wood-work, were as beautiful as their impressive exteriors. Mary Fraser remembered them affectionately as did everyone who travelled on them. She recalled, "In the 1930s we could get to Greenock from Hunter's Quay on a Saturday for 1/- return and to Glasgow for 2/6. We used to eat on the boat if we were having a short cruise. There was marvellous food on board. For lunch, for example, we would have soup, salmon or steak, plus dessert and coffee. The table was set with gleaming silver on lovely white linen tablecloths with linen napkins, and the service, by a white-coated steward, would be swift, friendly and excellent. Sometimes we would sail from Dunoon across to Rothesay, through the Kyles of Bute, or maybe around Arran. We loved sitting on deck and listening to the German band. We never really established if they were German, we just knew they were foreigners. They played all the current catchy tunes of the moment and then would go round the boat, hat in hand, for financial contributions. There were frequent sing-songs and the atmosphere was full of gaiety. It was marvellous."

David Beveridge had a different memory of those days. "One wintry Sunday evening when the last steamer for Gourock was attempting to berth at Dunoon pier in very inclement weather, the skipper decided to come alongside, stern first. Well, my father and another belated passenger thought they had missed the steamer and that she was leaving them stranded until the Monday morning, so they both made a terrific leap and landed on the heaving deck of the *Caledonia*. Strictly against regulations. Captain Dugald Cameron, a well-known pier-master, nearly burst an artery. My father managed to hide in the crowd but the other man was slower on his feet and was fined £1.00, a lot of money in those days."

Another winter's tale of that period concerns two Kilcreggan residents who arrived from Glasgow at Craigendoran pier after the steamer had berthed for the night. That popular and kindly Captain, Duncan Campbell, got his crew on deck and made an extra crossing to Kilcreggan.

The Clyde paddle steamers have always been of great service to the country in times of war, and at the beginning of the 1914-18 conflict various paddlers were requisitioned and used as troopships and mine-sweepers. *Kenilworth, Marmion, Glen Rosa, Jeanie Deans* and *King Edward* were just a few which saw active service.

During the 1939-45 war the steamers once again played their part, and at Dunkirk many of them could be seen making run after run up to the beach to collect the soldiers stranded there.After the war the paddlers returned to the Clyde but their demise was not far off.

In the early 1950s there were about twenty paddle steamers left plying the Clyde, and more than four million passengers were being carried by them during a good year. But British Rail insisted that they were no longer a paying proposition and plans were announced to close the 'small and unfrequented piers' around Loch Long and the Holy Loch. The days of the 'roll on, roll off' boats were coming and by the early 1980s Dunoon was left with just two car ferries; one run by Caledonian MacBrayne and the other by Western Ferries.

6

The War Years

DUNOON, AS WITH EVERY TOWN, village and city in the United Kingdom, was affected by the two World Wars.

In the 1914-18 war there was not much outward disturbance to everyday life, but the horror of the growing casualty lists affected every family in a place as small as Dunoon, where most people knew each other.

War was declared on a hot, sunny day, 4th August 1914. At the Pavilion and the Cosy Corner concert parties were in full swing and at the Burgh Hall played *The Man U Know* staged by the famous W.F. Frame. Mobilisation was already taking place for the 8th Argyll and Sutherland Highlanders, and a boom was soon to be stretched across the Clyde, from the Castle Rocks to the Cloch, to ensure that no enemy submarine could enter the river. Servicemen started to come into Dunoon and the Highland Light Infantry were stationed in the Pavilion and at Ardhallow Fort.

One night in October of that year, the officer in charge of the Fort heard that an enemy Zeppelin was seen over Edinburgh. Extremely worried about the possibility of it coming over Dunoon, he rushed to the Gas Works and ordered the gas supply to be immediately cut off, ensuring a complete blackout. As the town was solely lit by gas the suddenness of the switch-off caused great confusion. The shock was so severe to the inhabitants that one old lady died. The Cloch lighthouse-keeper, however, was not unduly worried as he thought that the disappearance of Dunoon's lights meant that sudden fog had descended. He therefore blasted his fog horn until the lights came on again!

On the 7th of May 1915 the world was shocked by the sinking of the great Cunard liner *Lusitania* by a German submarine off the coast of southern Ireland. She had been returning from New York to Liverpool when at 2pm a torpedo struck her. The liner disappeared under the sea in about twenty minutes. About thirteen hundred lives were lost, many of them American. Among the six hundred survivors were seven-year-old Francis Frankum and his father. The rest of the family were drowned. A few days after the sinking of the liner, a trunk belonging to the Frankums was washed ashore and sent to their home in Birmingham.

Frank was Clerk to the Cowal District Council and Registrar of Births until he retired, after almost fifty years in local government service.

Many local men and women were awarded honours in the war, most of them having been pupils of the Grammar School. A great number more were killed or wounded in that terrible conflict.

One to be honoured, and to survive, was Corporal William Angus Carluke. He was awarded the Victoria Cross for rescuing an officer, Lieutenant Martin, on the battlefield. In November 1915 he came home to crowds thronging the pier and lining the road to see him before he was honoured at the Argyll Hotel. Schoolchildren were given a day's holiday and there were enthusiastic celebrations in the town.

The arrival of a Russian ship, the *Askole*, in the Holy Loch caused quite a stir. She had five funnels and was therefore nicknamed the *Woodbine* because of the famous five-cigarette packet, so popular at the time.

Alex Waddell remembered being a young child when the ship came in round Ardnadam Pier. "The Russians were there for a short time," he recounted. "They could speak very little English. It was the time of the Revolution and at least the Captain was loyal to the Czar. The Royal Navy took over the ship and sent the Russians home via London. Luckily the Captain managed to escape, for there is no doubt he would have been shot if he had gone back. I know that one officer committed suicide rather than be sent back to Russia. The ship stayed in the loch for about two-and-a-half years and then was taken away to be broken up."

R. K. Arthur also had memories of the Russians' visit and the gaiety of some of the sailors. "The Russians were jolly 'Jack Tars' – nothing morose or sullen about them. The sailors were amazed at the simplest things like wristwatches, water-closets and, most of all, bicycles. I was on the spot when half-a-dozen of them came up to Young's hiring shop at the top of Wellington Street, near to where I lived. They hadn't a clue about riding them, but were eager and willing to learn. We helped them on the bikes but forgot to mention the brakes. They went down the steep hill like a skiing competition gone amuck, only able to stop by crashing into hedges and walls. The sailors rolled round hooting with laughter with their wee red touries bobbing about."

Armistice Day, 11th November 1918, was also recalled by R. K. Arthur. "A large bonfire was built on the Castle rocks at Sands' boating station which was to start a chain of fires along the coast. All

Dunoon Grammar School

The World War I boom across the Clyde from Dunoon to Cloch Point

For the first Christmas of World War II Provost Angus McFarlane (below) sent out 300 boxes of 'goodies' to local people serving with the Armed Forces. These had been paid for by a special War Fund

Dunoon Observer & Argyllshire Standard

was set for 9pm when the Provost, William Lees, was to set it alight. Alec Williamson and I were in position at Highland Mary's statue overlooking the gathering throng when we realised we each had two three-inch thunder flashes with strings. On an impulse of genius we fired across the road over the multitude of heads and one landed on the paraffin-soaked bonfire and set it alight. It blazed, and the other towns took heed and started their own bonfires. It was a pity when the Provost and Council arrived in open cabs an hour later to view a heap of ashes."

That morning, "The whole of the Grammar School was lined up to salute the Flag!" reminisced David Brechin. "There we were under Captain Lawrie who was in charge of the proceedings. Watching us with a sardonic grin was the old chap who sold fish from a wheelbarrow. The impressive moment came. Captain Lawrie gave the command: 'General Salute. Present Arms'. As we rattled our carbines to present, the band gave its preliminary blow and Captain Lawrie swirled round to salute the Flag. At that moment the fishmonger bawled out, 'Loch Fyne fresh herrings – this morning's fish.' It ruined the event, but made our day!"

This was the 'War to end all Wars', or so everyone thought. It was not to be. Twenty-one years later Great Britain again was at war with Germany.

Once more the boom stretched across the Firth. The Holy Loch became a submarine base and the biggest building in Dunoon, the Glasgow and West of Scotland Convalescent Homes was taken over by the Navy and renamed HMS *Osprey*. Lord Louis Mountbatten, then an Admiral of the Fleet, visited the Base during the early part of the war where thousands of officers and ratings were trained in Anti-Submarine Warfare (Asdic). Some people, to this day, claim that the Battle of the Atlantic was won in Dunoon!

Five hundred million tons of shipping was moved during the war by Clyde Trust Pilots and the Clyde was the centre of great activity.

James Napier remembered those days: "I was in the Royal Navy during the war and my first ship was HMS *Barbarian* on the boom from Dunoon to the Cloch. I spent eighteen happy months there and got to know Dunoon very well. The Glasgow Hotel was my favourite 'howff' and with many of the Argylls in prisoner-of-war camps we were very well received."

Dunoon was full of hundreds of evacuated children, sometimes with their mothers, and, of course, service men and women. Isabella MacVicar recalled those early days of the war. "HMS *Forth* was the first ship I remember coming in. She was a mother ship and she had the T Class of submarines. There were the *Truro, Trident, Thunderbolt* and *Thesus*. I remember a lady coming into my shop about this time. I asked her if she had come to stay in Dunoon. 'No,' she replied. 'My husband is on the *Forth*.' I told her I hoped she'd be happy here and she said, 'When I was leaving Rosyth, where I was staying while my husband was away, my landlady told me that if I was going to the West Coast I'd be ever so happy, for the people there are the salt of the earth.' "

In March 1941 there were heavy bombing raids on Clydebank, and the Dunoon side of the Firth had stray bombs dropped by bombers returning back to base. One of the first bombs was dropped near Inverchapel at the foot of Loch Eck, but no real damage was done. The attack took place on a moonlit night and the next day local children visited the spot in great excitement and carried off fragments of the bomb as souvenirs. There was also a bomb one night at Hunter's Quay and Mary Fraser remembered that night well: "The bomb struck a rock at the pier. It shattered about seven windows and brought a ceiling down. Glasgow and Greenock, of course, were very badly bombed that night, but I think it was just a pilot unloading his last bomb."

J. Gill remembered serving on HMS *Forth* when she sailed from Dunoon in 1940: "I think we sailed at dusk on a Friday evening arriving, as far as I can recall, sometime on the following Monday. Our passage round from Rosyth was, I am very glad to say, uneventful. In particular, through the Pentland Firth, the sea was flat and much in our favour from the point of view of U-boat spotting. The ship stayed on in Dunoon and I left her in September of 1940."

Besides HMS *Forth* there were another two depot ships in the Holy Loch – HMS *Titania* and HMS *Alrhoda* – each with its covey of submarines moored alongside. These would regularly slip out of the loch for a spell of duty in the Atlantic.

One day in August 1943 Sandbank, by the Holy Loch, had the shock of its life. The routine for submariners returning from duty was to check that all torpedo tubes were flooded with sea water, that the firing mechanisms operated properly and that everything was in good working order. Unfortunately someone had forgotten that the torpedo tube had an unfired torpedo in it. They began the drill and, to their horror, saw a live missile speed its way through a narrow gap between the many small moored craft and big ships anchored in the loch. Luckily the tide was such that the boats had their prows facing up the loch, for it would have been a disaster otherwise. There was an enormous explosion as the torpedo hit the foreshore, a hundred yards north of the jetty at the now demolished Robertson's Pier. Hundreds of panes of glass were shattered in the yard and in the neighbouring houses, and a hole, big enough to hold a house, was blasted in the sand.

One old lady buying milk from the horse-drawn milk cart was caught by the blast and blown right through the hedge. As she crawled out with the milk jug still firmly clasped in her hand she was heard to say to the bewildered milkman, "Your horse kicked me."

45

Douglas Stewart had a clear recollection of that August day: "A mighty column of assorted water, gravel and mussels, shot hundreds of feet into the blue sky. Nobody had been killed and none of the boats had been blown up. The only damage was a few dozen broken windows and a huge crater on the beach that was to be a fishing paradise for years until it silted up. Someone was fishing in a dinghy at the time. In some trepidation they saw the white wake of the torpedo heading straight for them but had no idea what it was. It had passed right under them as they sat petrified.

"My father was the village plumber and he had a splendid tale to tell of that morning. He was repairing the gutters on a house opposite the Post Office. An elderly lady came over and asked, 'Oh Mr Stewart, would you help me? I need to phone and it's yon new kind in the kiosk, with a dial to get the operator. I've never used one; could you phone for me?' 'Surely,' said my father, getting down from his steps. Halfway down them a thought struck him: No, I won't phone for her, for if I do she will be no better off, as she'll have to go looking for someone else to do it for her the next time. Instead, he decided to show her how it was done. They entered the phone box together and went over the instruction panel carefully. When he was sure she knew what to do my father left her to it and watched from across the road. Half a dozen times she read the instruction panel. She arranged her small change and then re-arranged it. She put her hand out towards the receiver then drew it back. Eventually she picked it up. The timing, according to my father, was immaculate! With a mighty roar the torpedo hit Sandbank. The old lady leapt out of the kiosk and tore off the road for home shouting, 'To hell with that! I'll send a postcard!' " (A fuller version of 'Sandbank's Big Bang' by Douglas L Stewart can be read in the May 1981 issue of *The Scots Magazine*.)

1942 was an eventful year, for the biggest gathering of any shipping ever was brought together on the Clyde ready for the Allies' invasion of North Africa – Operation Torch. Various stories circulated at that time, and one of the most amusing was that of the American officer just out of the States asking a stolid Scots policeman on the pierhead at Gourock where the urinal was. To this the policeman replied, "Now sir, you should know better than that. One mustn't mention ship's names here at a time like this, must we?"

At that time Isabella MacVicar's sister, Mary, was helping at the Tartan Club in the Burgh Hall. It was organised for service personnel and was a canteen as well as a social club. "Mary was always saying, 'Oh, have you nowhere to go? Just come back with me.' And she'd bring home young, lonely and homesick service men and women – just boys and girls really. They were so pleased to be part of a family again."

AILLST TB

On the **PS** *Waverley*, the last of the
paddle steamers to be seen on the
Clyde, can be seen the following plaque:

> This vessel replaces
> The Clyde steamer *Waverley*
> Which was built in 1899
> Served as a mine sweeper
> During the 1914–18 War
> And was sunk by enemy
> Action at Dunkirk on 1940.

Laura Doak, who was a Wren during the war, had very happy memories of being stationed in Dunoon where she was cherished by the Young family. Mrs Young made her so welcome in her home that Laura always regarded her as her Scottish mother. May McNeill, Mrs Young's daughter, lived in Dunoon in the 1980s and she and Laura saw each other whenever possible. "I remember crossing from Gourock in the river steamer *Queen Mary*," said Laura. "It was in January and the hills were covered in snow. I thought it was an enchanted place, and when a fellow-passenger pointed out the Holy Loch, I knew it must be. I remember, too, the loveliness of Dunoon itself and the beauty of the surrounding countryside, and last, but not least, the kindness of the Scottish people to the stranger in their midst.

"I remember going with another Wren from Toward to Rothesay and having tea in a café there. A man and his wife stopped at our table and he said he would pay our bill, as he knew how meagre our pay was.

"One day will always be in my memory. We had walked on a Sunday afternoon to Sandbank. Suddenly, turning down towards the loch was the loveliest sunset I had ever seen. The snow-covered hills were pink, and the sheer beauty took my breath away. The war seemed very far off."

It may have been at this time that the *Empire Haywood Stanhope*, a merchantman, sailed from Seville, in Spain, for the Clyde, carrying a cargo of marmalade and eating oranges. A German agent had planted a delayed-action bomb amongst the crates and the explosions began when the ship was in the Clyde. She dropped anchor off Hunter's Quay and bomb-disposal men came aboard to open all the crates in case of more explosives. The oranges were rolled down chutes into lighters. Many dropped into the sea and floated ashore with different tides on both sides of the estuary. The village policeman near the moored vessel heard two very small boys, obviously with no memories of the fruit, hold one up and say, "If it bounces its a baw, if it explodes it's a bomb."

In 1943 the song *Bonnie Dunoon* was launched on behalf of local War charities. It was written and composed by Pipe Major John McLellan DCM, author of *Cowal Gathering* and many other well-known bagpipe airs, and an early holder for solo piping of the Dunoon Burgh Cup.

May 8th 1945 saw the end of hostilities in Europe. Church bells pealed joyously all over the country and Thanksgiving Services were held in packed places of worship.

By the end of August the war with Japan ended and the world struggled to get back to a peaceful existence. However the Clyde was still the scene of activity with great warships coming and going, and

Dunoon Observer & Argyllshire Standard

Dunoon & Cowal's tradition of military service is evident in this photo of two Dunoon soldiers reading their local paper
The *Dunoon Observer & Argyllshire Standard* came into its own as a true community leader during World War II and was a symbol of defiance by local people against the enemy, never missing an edition, even though rationing necessitated its size being cut to just a single broadsheet printed on both sides

49

troopships bearing more American servicemen.

There was a great 'Welcome Home' for five hundred local men and women who had been demobilised from the services. HMS *Osprey* was disbanded and the following year the Cowal Highland Gathering took place after suspension during the war. The big stocks of bunting, flags, tartans and clan shields which had been bought just before the outbreak of the war for that year's Games were in constant demand by other towns and burghs in Scotland, owing to the ever-present post-war shortages.

Sadly there were to be other skirmishes and wars at various ends of the earth to which local men and women went – Korea, Malaya and Aden, to name just a few. And, of course, more recently four Dunoon men, Malcolm MacKinnon, Donald MacAleese, Francis Guichan and Graham Turnbull joined the Task Force to liberate the Falkland Islands. On their return they were given a reception at Castle House where they were presented with inscribed tankards.

To commemorate the two hundred and fifty-five men and three women who died in the Falklands war, the same number of white heather plants, shipped from The White Heather Farm at Toward, were planted on the slopes near Port Stanley where the final battle took place. A bronze plaque marks the spot and gives the origin of the heather.

Just nine years after the Falklands, war erupted again in the Gulf. In January 1991 the Dunoon detachment of 205 General Hospital consisting of Cathy and Janet Anderson, Jimmy Love and his two sons, James (wee Jimmy) and David, Stuart McLean and Helen McVicar, flew out to Riyadh, Saudi Arabia, to join the forces of 'Operation Storm'. After two months in the Gulf the Dunoon personnel came home. Subsequently they were presented with medals from the British and Saudi governments.

7

Uncle Sam Arrives

NO SOONER had the Americans left Dunoon after the war that it seemed that they were back – this time as 'peace keepers' for the NATO Alliance.

On 1st November 1960, the Conservative Prime Minister, Harold Macmillan, announced, "There would be an operational advantage, and the deterrent would thereby be strengthened if sheltered anchorage on this side of the Atlantic could be provided for a submarine depot and floating dock, and that Her Majesty's Government have undertaken to provide this anchorage in the Holy Loch."

Despite massive assurances from the authorities that there would be no danger from the nuclear reactors in the submarines, that there would be no restrictions on sailing in the Holy Loch, and that the holders of the peace-keeping deterrent would not impinge too much on the indigenous population, shock and distress reverberated through the area.

It was initially agreed that the first submarines due into the Holy Loch in March 1961 would be the flagship of the squadron of nine. The only shore establishments would be a small jetty on the loch for tenders, and warehouses at Greenock for storage purposes. It was also agreed that no more than three submarines at a time would be lying in the loch. The US originally planned to base fifteen hundred men on the depot ship USS *Proteus* and at least four hundred of them were expected to bring their families. There were to be no special houses built for them but plans were made for rented accommodation on both sides of the Firth. In the event, the Post Office Pension Fund financed the building of a large complex of houses for the use of American servicemen and their families near Sandbank.

The week before the *Proteus* sailed into the Holy Loch the world's press descended on Dunoon. The event was so important that CBS ran a half-hour programme for American television when the ship eventually arrived.

Alex Waddell and his daughter, Eileen Lea, had memories of that day: "There were terrific demonstrations by the CND. It was a very high tide and fairly stormy, so a ferryboat was chartered to bring the demonstrators into Hunter's Quay, where they came along the Shore Road in droves. Some of them were really weird – hippies, unwashed and unshaven. The police were drafted in aplenty and they herded and pushed the demonstrators down the shore of our place. It was certainly the biggest demonstration we had ever seen. Of course, there was no water, no cooking and no sanitation facilities, so you can imagine what the place was like. The police simply didn't know what to do with the enormous number of people."

There were mixed feelings about the arrival of the Americans despite the fact that there had been thousands stationed in the area during the two World Wars. Some of the sailors were greeted with warmth and made to feel welcome, while others were rejected by a vocal minority and, of course, there was no doubt that the local people were apprehensive and uncertain about their, and the district's future. Their worries proved to be unfounded for the Americans in Dunoon and its environs kept a very low profile. One permanent reminder that the place was full of servicemen was the queue of taxis at Ardnadam Pier and outside the Burgh Hall in Dunoon.

Important visitors to the area usually made the Submarine Base a port of call. In June 1978, Lord Louis Mountbatten, a member of the Royal Family, one of Britain's most distinguished naval officers, and the last Viceroy of India, came to present the Battenburg Cup aboard the USS *Holland*. Little did anyone present at that impressive ceremony think that, just over a year later, Lord Louis would have been murdered by the IRA whilst fishing with his family on his little boat off the coast of Ireland.

April 1981 was the twentieth anniversary of the US Naval presence in the Holy Loch. The occasion was celebrated in the Loch Ness Room at the Shore Base at Ardnadam. The principal guest was Sir Fitzroy MacLean, the well-known writer, soldier, diplomat and former MP. The special cake was cut with a highland dirk by Sir Fitzroy while Captain Guy Curtis, Commodore of Submarine Squadron 14, used his navy cutlass.

Those thirty years of the American presence in Dunoon saw much adjustment on both sides. There were many marriages to local girls and a great deal of participation by the American personnel and their families in local events. The number of personnel employed at the base was, of course, far larger than originally stated, with some 3000 service people plus their families on station at any one time. The children of servicemen and women attended local schools and many lifelong friendships were made in this way. As a means of saying 'thank you' to the

The **NATO** Base on the Holy Loch
showing the dry dock, Polaris
submarines and submarine tender.
Local people were surprised at the
sheer scale of the **US** presence but
during the thirty-one years of their stay
became used to it. During the Cuban
missile crisis of 1962, the depot ship
USS *Proteus* disappeared for a secret
destination

local population the US Navy, every spring, invited the general public on board the submarine tender. Visitors were transported by liberty boats from Ardnadam Pier for an organised tour of the ship. It was an exciting experience to look down from the great height of the ship's bridge to see the anchored yachts and sailing dinghies looking very small on the loch, and to view the magnificent hills in the spring sunshine from such an excellent vantage point.

In February 1991 the US Navy announced that it was to close its Base on the Holy Loch. Once again the local community was divided as to whether the Navy's departure would be detrimental or advantageous to Dunoon. It was hard to escape the fact that any advantages would be in the long term, whereas the immediate future would entail a loss of something in the region of £11million a year and at least 850 jobs.

Luis Llovet, an American from San Juan, Puerto Rico, had come to Scotland as a twenty-two year old sailor. He loved the area so much that he served ten consecutive years on the Holy Loch, marrying a Scots lass during that time. Luis remembered learning the news of the intended closure of the Base on BBC television an hour before being told by his commanding officer! The closure took place much more quickly than anyone had expected. A year later, almost to the day, thirty years of dollar subsidy ended. Luis Llovet was part of the Base's decommissioning team. He was Petty Officer in charge of the dry dock vessel, *Los Alamos*. When it left the loch initially to be anchored at Greenock, he was involved in a unique operation involving the world's largest lifting ship, the Dutch *Mighty Servant III*. That vessel had to take on board the floating dock that was used during Polaris submarine refits and take her across the Atlantic. Some barges and a huge crane were still in the Holy Loch and these were shipped to another Base in Sardinia. To Luis Llovet's amazement the tug boats that came to collect them were from San Juan, Puerto Rico. The circle, as far as Luis was concerned, had been completed.

About three or four months after the Base had closed, and on two separate occasions, a couple of US sailors were sent to the Holy Loch for duty. As they were unable to find a single sign of any naval presence they had to ask at the police station where the Base could be found. No one had told them it had been closed!

Some years before the eventual withdrawal of the US Navy from the Holy Loch in 1992, the houses that had been built to accommodate naval personnel and their families were bought by a property company. After the closure of the base, these houses were renovated and the area around them landscaped. Sandhaven, as it is now called, is an attractive housing development on the north shore of the Holy Loch and a fitting reminder of Dunoon's American years.

USS *Simon Lake,* **the last ship of the US
Navy to leave the Holy Loch in March
1992**
**This was a poignant moment for
everyone, whatever their feelings had
been about the US presence. An era
had ended**

Cowal Highland Gathering Ltd

One of the many pipe bands walking proudly along Argyll Street to take their part in the Cowal Highland Gathering held in Dunoon stadium

8

Cowal Highland Gathering

ONE OF THE great annual events that takes place in Dunoon on the last Friday and Saturday in August is the Cowal Highland Gathering.

Over thirty thousand people (a great number from overseas) flock to the town's sports stadium to watch this marvellous display of all the ancient Scottish sports such as tossing the caber, throwing the hammer, putting the shot, pole vaulting, and all the other events associated with Highland Games.

The two main features of the Cowal Highland Gathering are the World's Championship Pipe Band Contest and the Highland dancing. Anyone who has been at the gathering will know the enormous enjoyment derived from watching the various skills on display. And it would be a very unromantic person indeed who could watch, quite unmoved, the two thousand or more pipers and drummers march down the hill into the crowded stadium and on through the town.

Long ago the Gaels used to hold sports gatherings before the autumn crops had been safely gathered in, and from these meetings, which became a feature of Highland social life, grew the immensely popular Games of today. An interesting, though highly unlikely, origin of the Games is that a local ruler, being dissatisfied with the performance of his messengers, held races up steep hills, awarding the first home with a purse filled with gold, and the runner-up with a sword.

There has always been a great love of sport in the Dunoon area. In the mid 1800s a championship prize fight took place behind Kirn at Ardenslate on the Roman camp site. The contest was between a Glasgow publican, John Goudie, and an Irishman, Ned Langlands. It was an icy winter's morning, yet over two thousand people came to watch it. Most of them arrived from Glasgow and the piermaster had great difficulty in extracting from the visitors the twopence pier dues.

Reports of the fight vary – some say Goudie was fouled by Langlands after a few rounds and that Langlands disappeared into the crowd because he was worried about its reactions; others say that Goudie was the victor.

One eye-witness, Peter McPherson, a boatman, many years later gave his own version of the fight. He said, "Goudie had given Langlands a sair hammerin and Goudie had then leaped ower the ropes and made off because the Irish in the crowd were furious at his victory."

After the fight the shopkeepers shut up their shops and the pier was guarded with strong men wielding oak sticks, for there was only one policeman in Dunoon in those days.

In the 1880s Dunoon formed an amateur rowing club which was considered to be one of the best in Scotland. The crew once carried their boat on their shoulders from Arrochar to Tarbet, launched it on Loch Lomond, won the championships, and then carried the boat the same way, back to Arrochar, where they boarded a steamer to sail home to Dunoon.

It was not long before someone had the idea of having Highland Games in Dunoon. In 1894 Robert Cameron (known locally as 'the crofter') with some of his friends, sent out invitations to pipers and athletes in the area to compete in a contest of skills at the Glebe. Not many people turned up, so the bellman, Elliott, was sent round the town to proclaim that admission had fallen from one shilling to six-pence. It was of no use. The meeting was a complete disaster.

Undeterred, the organisers, without Cameron who had gone north, tried again and in 1900 the venue was changed to Ardenslate Park. This time a big publicity campaign to promote the Games was launched and the main attraction was to be a lady parachutist jumping from a balloon over the Park. This event brought out hundreds of folk and the Games were a great success.

Major J. D. Outram, whose name is synonymous with the early Gatherings, was elected the Games' first chairman in 1903. It was his excellent idea to feature a Pipe Band contest. Princess Louise (one of Queen Victoria's daughters) wife of the Duke of Argyll, the first Chieftain of the Gathering, helped design the Argyll Shield, which is still a coveted award at the band contest.

When Harry Lauder, the famous Scots singer-comedian, came to live in Dunoon, he suggested that the contest should extend to civilian bands, and he presented the Lauder Targe, now known as the Lauder Shield, as a first prize.

In the early days a well-known Games judge was Donald Dinnie. Dinnie, born in 1837, was a Scottish professional athlete with immense versatility and power. He was a first-class wrestler, weight-lifter, high-jumper, and excelled in the shot and hammer events.

On the eve of the Games the big social event for the county was a Grand Ball held at the Pavilion.

Cowal Highland Gathering Ltd

No longer just hopeful, these young lassies have won their trophies for Highland dancing

The 1914-18 war put a stop to the Games but they were resumed in 1919. However, the Games that year were a sad affair as it was evident how many of the participants of previous years had been killed or wounded in the war, for only eight bands were able to take part.

Among early competitors were Bob Vogt, a well-known Scottish cyclist who once had his bicycle collapse under him; the runner, Dr John Ritchie, a local doctor whose father was a coachman at Hafton; Pipe Major John McLellan, composer of *The Road to the Isles* and *Bonnie Dunoon*; and Pipe Major John Macdougall Gillies of Glendaruel, the first man to win the Cowal Gold Medal and to lead his band to win the Argyll Shield.

One of Scotland's most popular athletes was Duncan McLeod Wright, winner of the 1929 Marathon at the Olympic Games, a performance he repeated in 1939 at the First Empire Games in Canada, where he won by an amazing half-mile length. 'Dunky', as he was called by his friends, used to take part in the Games before the Second World War, and for many years afterwards announced the results, as he knew most of the competitors personally by name. In 1958 he became President of the Scottish Amateur Athletic Association and played a large part in the planning of the 1970 Commonwealth Games in Edinburgh. Barbara McConnochie, a keen Highland dancer who used to compete at the post-war Games, remembered an occasion in the 1950s when 'Dunky' was brought to the stadium by helicopter.

A. J. Watt's holidays used to coincide with Cowal Highland Gathering and he recalled one year when he was there. "It was 1927 and Sir Harry Lauder, as usual wearing his kilt, made a presentation to 'Jocky' Cunningham, the racing cyclist. Afterwards, Sir Harry mounted the bicycle for photographs to be taken. Someone gave him a push and Sir Harry completed a lap much to the delight of the spectators."

Two years later another sporting event was inaugurated in Dunoon – the Cloch to Dunoon swim. The first swim was won by a Glasgow policemen, William Burns, who competed against the popular American Zittenfield twins.

Daisy Boyce mentioned that her friend Violet Dickson (neé Anderson) competed in the event and, three years later, was the first person to swim from Dunoon to the Cloch and back in the very fast time of 2 hours 55 minutes. Violet also held the record for a swim from Rothesay to Dunoon – a distance of 15 miles – when she swam between the two towns in 1930 in a time of 8 hours 11 minutes.

G. Hughes remembered Edward Temme, the first man to swim the channel both ways, taking part in one of the early Cloch–Dunoon events. When Temme was being helped out of the water by Mr Hughes' uncle he said, "It was just a little bit of practice." The swim used to be an annual event until the first death occurred in 1946, to be followed by another, seven years later. It was then that the decision was taken to give up the event.

In the 1930s, associated with the Games, were competitions for original tunes. Entries came from all parts of the Empire and the competition proved so successful that a book containing the best hundred entries was immediately sold out.

In 1938, for the very first time, Dunoon was decorated during Games week with bunting and flags. Tartan banners, with the appropriate clan shields above them, were mounted on long poles all along the main street and were a source of interest and admiration.

The following year was the last of the games until 1946. War had intervened once more. On their revival the Games were as popular as ever and in August 1950, 30,000 people attended on the Saturday alone.

John McFall remembered that year very well. As a schoolboy he spent many of his summer holidays with relatives in Dunoon and they usually took him to see the Games. He recalled that the Labour Prime Minister, Clement Attlee, later to become Earl Attlee, attended on the Saturday when Mrs Attlee presented the main prizes. In the evening the Attlees were entertained by Provost Edward Wyatt at the Royal Marine Hotel, Hunter's Quay.

Nowadays, on the Thursday before the Games there is a traditional Sunset Ceremony in Argyll Gardens. Usually performed by Scouts and Boys Brigade lads and other youngsters who are taking part in the Games, the evening's entertainment is movingly ended by 'Beating the Retreat' and 'Lights Out'.

The finale of the Cowal Highland Gathering is, of course, the outstanding fireworks display at the coal jetty which is always attended by several thousand people.

9

'That's Entertainment'

FROM THE TIME that the gardens of Dunoon's Castle House were opened to the public in 1893 by Sir William Arrol, they were for many years the centre of Dunoon's entertainment.

The gardens were even a meeting place for illegal gamblers, and in the early 1900s a Glaswegian was imprisoned for twenty days because he was unable to pay his £2 fine for playing 'banker'.

Before the Pavilion was built in 1905 indoor entertainment took place in the Burgh Hall. The Pavilion, built on the site of the existing Queen's Hall, was opened by the Duke of Argyll and HRH Princess Louise. The first place of entertainment of its kind in Scotland, it was an excellent example of the best Victorian architecture, though some of its fine lines were lost by the addition of a roof-garden above the entrance, and tea-rooms and toilets on one side.

There was a splendid dance-floor which had room for at least 800 dancers at one time, and for those less enthusiastic there was a large spectators' gallery. During the season, except for Sunday which was rigidly kept as a day of observance, there were daily concerts featuring internationally renowned artistes.

Henry Rushbury, whose family settled in Scotland in the 1850s, told of his father's uncle, W. T. Rushbury, who used to come regularly to Dunoon to entertain. At nineteen W. T. became accompanist to the famous Helen Kirk and toured all over Scotland with her. Then he joined the celebrated comic-vocalist and sketch artiste, Arthur Lloyd, who pioneered the touring concert-party. Eventually he formed his own theatrical company touring Scotland with such plays as *The Old Home* and *Murder in the Red Barn*. Henry's father and uncle used to travel ahead, booking accommodation and seeing to the printing of tickets and bills. At one time W. T. lived in Dunoon and whenever he was practising at home playing and singing (he had a fine baritone voice) folk used to gather outside his window to listen to him. W. T. died in Airdrie but, according to his wishes, was buried in Dunoon.

T & R Annan

The Pavilion, built on the present site of its replacement, the Queen's Hall, was opened in 1905 by the Duke of Argyll and HRH Princess Louise. An excellent example of Victorian architecture, it was the first place of entertainment of its kind in Scotland with a seating capacity of 2500. The Pavilion burned down in the early hours of 3rd April 1949 when most of the building was destroyed

Besides the Pavilion, Cosy Corner and Burgh Hall, Dunoon was soon to have two more places of entertainment. The first cinema, La Scala, was built in 1913 and owned by the man who began the Glasgow Green Music Hall, and the second was The Picture House, both cinemas situated in Argyll Street.

During the years many famous artistes appeared in shows at Dunoon: Scottish-born Cissie Loftus, daughter of another famous music-hall star, Marie Loftus, was a marvellous mimic and a star attraction wherever she appeared; Charles Coburn, who gave the music hall two of its greatest songs, *Two Lovely Black Eyes* and *The Man Who Broke the Bank at Monte Carlo* ; Norman Long, whose catchphrase 'A song, a smile and a piano' became popular; and the famous principal boy, Phyllis Dare. Another great success in Dunoon was the Saltcoats impresario, Harry Kemp, with his 'Sunny Joy Company'.

There was a wealth of comedy too. Famous Scots comedians who had made their names in the theatres of Edinburgh and Glasgow came to entertain at Dunoon and other Clyde holiday resorts. There were artistes such as Charlie Kemble, Dave Willis and Alan Melville, later to make a name for himself as a comedy writer.

Two of the many artistes, still household names, who came to Dunoon to entertain during the season, were Jack Buchanan and John McCormack. Buchanan, the Helensburgh-born musical-comedy actor with his dashing and debonair style, was to find fame in movies both in Britain and in Hollywood. The records of John McCormack, with his fine tenor voice, are now collectors' pieces.

A unique year for Dunoon was 1928 when the town celebrated its Diamond Jubilee as a Burgh. The highlight of the Civic Week was the Historical Pageant held in the Recreational Park. In nine episodes, a cast of five hundred presented the history of Dunoon from earliest days up to 1868 when the Burgh was created. The opening performance was an enormous success attracting about 8,000 spectators.

That year Margaret Botting who, in the 1950s and '60s was a frequent contributor to the BBC's *Woman's Hour,* was spending her holiday with an aunt in Dunoon. She was a young girl then and remembered hearing Webster Booth, the tenor and light comedian, when he appeared in a summer concert-party in the open air bandstand in the Castle Gardens. Margaret said, "I sat there enraptured and quite fell in love with him." One of his numbers was *Take a Pair of Sparkling Eyes* and even then I recognised the star quality which proved itself in subsequent years when he and his wife, Anne Ziegler, became the leading variety and radio duetists of the 1940s and '50s."

Margaret also remembered the amateur singing contests which were a popular feature of the concert-party world in those days, and on the finals night the Pavilion was always packed.

Castle Gardens, Dunoon,

(above) Crowds enjoying public entertainment at Dunoon's Castle Gardens bandstand – a common sight before the advent of foreign package holidays

(below) Catering for all tastes – Dick Sutherd's Merry Geishas, pictured here in 1909, performed at the Cosy Corner on the site of Dunoon's present swimming pool. The company filled the Cosy Corner to capacity season after season with a show that was as popular with locals as visitors

Talent contests were also recollected by May Gallacher: "Herman Dimskie, the one-time famous band leader, used to play at the Pavilion at weekends and hold talent contests for persons of all ages. Singers, tap-dancers and sopranos all competed, and there were also leg competitions for men and women. I sang the number one song of the time, *Oh You Beautiful Doll* , and won £1."

One of the most genial, generous and well-loved men in Dunoon was Dick Sutherd whose famous 'Merry Geishas' filled the Cosy Corner to capacity season after season. 'Uncle Dick.' as he was affectionately known, used to create quite a stir locally when he rode his white horse through the town.

Stuart Peck had memories of the little concert hall which was on the site now occupied by the swimming pool: "It was really no more than a corrugated iron building with a simple trodden earth floor inside. During the season, when a lot of children were present, there were the usual shouted interruptions and continuous whispering."

Donald MacVicar remembered Uncle Dick with great affection: "He was a wonderful man and his shows were wonderful too. When he first started the Cosy Corner it was in a big tent at the corner of Moir Street and Alexandra Parade. The boys in his company wore white flannels and double-breasted jackets with brass buttons and sailing caps. The girls all wore sailor suits with frilled skirts. The troupe was hand-picked and was with him all season." Donald also mentioned various artistes who came to Dunoon. "I remember Donald Peers making a great impression on his audience with his song, *By a Babbling Brook*. Little did we think in those days that he would be a number one singing star in the 1950s, still with that song. Then there was Jack Anthony who sang Scottish songs accompanied by his wife. They were called 'Mr and Mrs Glasgow'. The Aberdonian, Harry Gordon, was another great favourite. He was a marvellous comedian and one of Scotland's great pantomime stars. His show *Harry Gordon's Entertainers* ran from 1924-40 in Aberdeen. He was a regular broadcaster and I'll never forget his song, *Bunty Pulls The Strings* ."

David Beveridge was another fan of Uncle Dick's and had great memories of the many famous artistes he saw at the Cosy Corner. In particular he remembered Renée and Billie Houston, who soon were to establish themselves in the leading London and provincial music halls. After Billie retired, Renée, who became a famous character actress as well as a radio and television personality, worked a new double act with her husband, Donald Stewart.

Other stars David enjoyed going to see were Tommy Lorne, the comedian whose revue *Froth* was a great success in 1924 at Glasgow's Pavilion Theatre, Ike Freedman, Jack Radcliffe and Dave Willis who was famous for *I'm the smartest warden in the ARP* .

The Bathing Lido, Dunoon. 14388.

Dunoon's bathing lido was built in the 1930s. Its site on the East Bay was not popular for swimming. After it was closed it was taken over as a pottery, before it was finally demolished

E. B. Macintyre met George Formby and his wife Beryl just before the Second World War. They often used to come to Dunoon for a holiday but it is not known if Formby ever performed in the town. Formby made his stage debut in 1921 and with his toothy grin and famous ukulele became a popular singing comedian. His most famous songs were *When I'm Cleaning Windows* and *Leaning On A Lamp-post* .

The town suffered a terrible blow in 1949 when, in the early hours of Sunday 3rd April, the Pavilion burnt down. Despite heroic attempts by Dunoon's Fire Brigade, aided by a fire-float from Greenock, most of the building was destroyed. With only a few months to go before the summer season the Council was desperate. However, it had the brilliant idea of buying two Blister hangars from the Fleet Air Arm stationed at Stranraer and, put together, these were able to seat over one thousand people as well as accommodate over six hundred dancers. It was not a perfect solution but it served the town as a major place of entertainment until the new Pavilion was ready by the spring of 1958. In fact, one of the most successful Mods (festivals) of *An Comunn Gaidhealach* was held in it.

The new Pavilion was officially opened on 25th April by the Rt. Hon John S. Maclay, Secretary of State for Scotland, and renamed The Queen's Hall on 11th August after the Queen and Prince Philip's visit to Dunoon.

Bringing Dunoon's tradition for live entertainment up to date, in October 1992 a Jazz Festival was inaugurated in the town. Concerts now take place annually in the Queen's Hall and at many other venues.

10

Sir Harry Lauder

IF THERE WAS one person who made the name of Dunoon known throughout the world, it was Sir Harry Lauder. The first Scots entertainer to become an international star, this small, stocky, marvellously gifted man, entertained audiences by comic patter and amusing anecdotes.

Harry Lauder was born on 4th August 1870 at Portobello, then a coastal village, near Edinburgh. His father, John Lauder, was always very proud of being the son of a Lauder of Lauderdale, a district of the Borders famous for song and story in Scottish history, and in turn Harry was imbued with this pride and affection for the district.

Harry's mother was a MacLellan from the Black Isle, Ross-shire, who came from real Highland stock, and it was from her that he inherited his love of Highland lore and romance.

John Lauder, a potter in Musselburgh making ginger-pop bottles and jelly jars, died when Harry was only twelve years old. The family moved to Arbroath where Mrs Lauder had some relatives and, as the eldest of seven children, Harry had a great responsibility to the family who were often very near the breadline. He found a job as a half-timer in one of Arbroath's flax mills. This meant alternate days at work and at school. His mother had insisted on his joining the local teetotal Band of Hope and at their meetings usually one of the children was asked to sing or recite. One night young Harry got up shyly to sing *I'm a Gentleman Still* which proved a huge success with his audience. After that the boy would usually win first prize in any amateur singing competition that he entered.

After two years in Arbroath the family moved to Hamilton, some twelve miles outside Glasgow, the centre of one of the greatest coal-mining areas in Britain. Harry went to work down the mine.

The underground manager of the mine where Harry worked was James Vallance, whose son Tom was a friend of his. It was through Tom that Harry met the one and only love of his life, Annie, always

(right) Harry Lauder in unfamiliar style – a portrait drawn for a feature in the Glasgow periodical, the *Bailie*

(below left) With his friend Sir Thomas Lipton on board ship bound for New York

(below right) Sir Thomas Lipton in the doorway of his home at Osidge with his Daimler and Panhard motor cars. He kept a fleet of cars for the use of his friends. During seasons in London theatres, Lauder often stayed with Sir Thomas and drove in his cars to performances

Mitchell Library

called Nance. Harry and Nance were married on 18th June 1890 and spent a singularly curious honeymoon. They had a day in Glasgow, most of which was spent looking at the waxworks at MacLeod's, Trongate. Later on they went on the top of a tramcar to the gates of Barlinnie Prison!

At this time the young Lauder was in great demand to sing at local concerts all round the district with, usually, a prize to be won. As his reputation grew, so did the invitations. During this period he sang mostly ballads and burlesque songs that had been featured by other singers, but soon he adapted and rewrote many of them adding his own brand of comedy patter.

Mrs Baylis, who owned the Scotia, the oldest music hall in Scotland (opposite Glasgow's Fish Market) enjoyed encouraging new talent, so engaged Lauder for a week. It was all very well having the odd week's stage work, but Harry had to decide if this was to be his career. Soon afterwards he was lucky to be offered a six-weeks engagement from the Kennedys, a well-known couple who organised concert tours round the small Scottish towns. Although he was a success, there were no more offers when the tour finished and he felt, as a married man with a wife to support, that he would have to go back to the pit for a regular income. Just as he was thinking of returning to the mine he was asked to appear for a week during the New Year at Greenock Town Hall. Those seven days were a nightmare for the singer. The Greenock and Port Glasgow riveters and engineers rolled up in their hundreds for the performances but hissed and booed so persistently that Harry decided to give up the stage and remain a miner.

However, the lure of the theatre proved too great, and after a short spell back in the pit he accepted an offer for a month's tour of halls in the north of England, finishing up with a couple of weeks at the Scotia and Gaiety Theatre in Glasgow.

This was the turning point in Lauder's career. He decided to make a feature of being a Scottish comedian and prove himself an exceptionally successful one. He worked hard to improve his repertoire and at the end of his tour he had plenty of offers for further engagements. At last he was a *real* performer.

His London debut, when he was thirty, was at Gatti's-in-the-Road where he was an immediate success. Soon he was acknowledged as a star and appeared in all the important music halls in the capital.

At that period every leading artiste made one West-End appearance a night, filling in the remainder of the evening by appearing in two, three, or even four, suburban music halls. Before the days of motor cars the 'top of the bill' would hire a private cab or a two-horse brougham to take him, or her, to the different places of entertainment. Sometimes it was 'touch and go' whether the driver would be able to arrive at the hall on time and often an earlier turn would have to extend his act until the star arrived.

When Lauder bought his first motor car, a small coupé, with an engine that chugged like a locomotive, his brother-in-law and faithful friend (later his manager) Tom Vallance, chauffeured him all over London and the suburbs without Harry missing a turn by more than a minute or two. Sometimes he played four halls a night, two of them twice, when the double programme was introduced.

When Lauder sang his most famous song *I Love A Lassie* it became an immediate hit, and suddenly he realised that he had engagements booked for years ahead. He began recording his songs and his gramophone records sold as successfully as any of today's pop stars.

In the middle of October 1907 Lauder went on his first American tour. He was as great a success in the States as he was in Britain and his career progressed through the years with engagements at home and overseas.

In 1909 Lauder bought a large house, Gerhallow, in Bullwood, Dunoon, renaming it Lauderdale after the district in the Borders. He built a high wall around the grounds to give him and his family privacy, for he was fast becoming a famous personality. Locally, he was a familiar figure driving with Nance or his son John in a small phaeton coach drawn by a little piebald pit pony. Isabella MacVicar (née Black) remembered that no one in Bullwood ever paid much attention to Harry Lauder because they never considered him, at that time, to be very important. "I used to walk three miles to Dunoon Grammar School and when John would see me coming he waited for me. He had one of the first Fords with the wee seat at the back. He used to open the lid over the dicky seat, and he would put me in, and there would be letters on the seat. I knew I had to take these and post them in the pillar-box outside the school."

In 1910 Harry Lauder played in pantomime in Glasgow and there introduced another great hit, *Roamin' in the Gloamin'* .

Two of Harry Lauder's closest friends were Sir Thomas Lipton and Willie Blackwood. During London engagements he would stay either with Willie at his home in Harrow or, more frequently, with Lipton at Osidge.

In *Leaves from the Lipton Logs* Sir Thomas describes his good friend: "Jocularly he used to say that he got better attention at our houses then he got in any hotel. 'And besides,' he would add with that little twinkle in his eye, 'it's much cheaper!'

"I don't know what Harry did at Harrow, but at Osidge he simply took command of the house. He was very particular about his meals and ordered just what he wanted at certain specified hours, whether these were the regulation meal hours at Osidge or not. It was very amusing to hear him give his pointed instructions to John, one of my Cingalese servants.

" 'At six o'clock sharp, to the second, John, you old rascal, I want ham and eggs, dry toast, and weak tea – without any milk in it! Ham well frizzled and the eggs done on both sides – do you understand? And tell Baker to have the car waiting for me at six-twenty sharp. And that's a' the noo, John!'

"John would stand like a graven image while Sir Harry was giving his instructions and when the famous little comedian was finished, he would bow solemnly and reply, 'Very good, Sir Harry. I got it all here' pointing to his head. I sometimes thought that John and the other servants were not very sure who was 'boss o' the hoose' at such times – Sir Harry Lauder or myself!"

The years went by and Harry was so busy fulfilling his British and American commitments that he was only able to get away to his home in Dunoon for the occasional weekend.

In 1914 Harry, taking Nance with him, went on a tour of Australia. John, who had been training as a subaltern in the Territorial Regiment of the 8th Argyllshire Battalion, Argyll and Sutherland Highlanders, was to join them for a long holiday during the summer vacation from Cambridge, where he was studying music. He was with his parents on his father's birthday, 4th August, and heard of the outbreak of war. The next day he was ordered to rejoin his regiment and sailed for England leaving behind his parents, as Harry had several engagements until the spring of 1915.

When Harry and Nance returned home they saw a lot of John, who was stationed in England with the 51st division of the Argyll and Sutherland Highlanders. This division was almost unique in the British Army. Being a territorial unit, officers and men were well-known to each other and were more like brothers and friends.

During that same year the Lauders returned to the States, Harry spending most of the time involved in propaganda in the hope that the Americans would enter the war. They returned home early in 1916 in time to welcome John, now a captain, home on his first leave from France.

In the summer of that year John became engaged to Mildred Thomson, whose father owned a big warehouse in London. They had actually known each other as children in Scotland where their parents had lived relatively near each other. But it was not until they met in London that they fell in love.

Harry, with his son's future in mind, bought Glenbranter, a large and comfortable mansion house on a beautiful estate in one of the loveliest parts of Argyll, with enough land to build a house for John and Mildred when they were married.

Sir Harry Lauder's House, Dunoon.

323/128

Lauderdale, Bullwood, Dunoon was bought by Sir Harry Lauder in 1908. It was an impressive house full of beautiful furniture and numerous mementoes of Harry Lauder's many overseas tours. David Beveridge remembered Sir Harry flying the Union Jack upside down on a flagpole in the garden for a whole summer despite many angry letters from sea captains pointing out that this was a distress signal

In 1934 the Lauders left Lauderdale for a house at Strathaven. Lauderdale became a private hotel and was burned down on 28th March 1962 resulting in the death of the owner

In June the regiment went to Ripon. R. K. Abram, 'Bunny' to all his many friends, was a brother-officer of John Lauder. He remembered that Harry was playing at a theatre in Leeds at the time and came over to the Mess to dine. After dinner the Colonel asked him to sing, and for the very first time he sang in public *O'er the hills tae Ardentinny, Just tae see ma bonnie Jeannie* .

Later in the year the regiment went back to France. Bunny was then a 2nd Lieutenant, and the Lewis Gun officer, at Battalion Head-quarters at Courcelette on the Somme. Conditions were terrible that winter and it was so wet that the Highlanders had to remove their kilts and wear trews and thigh gumboots to enable them to cope with the terrain. The potholes were so deep and full of water that some men actually drowned in them. One morning the message came in that Captain John Lauder had been killed.

Harry Lauder was playing in London to packed audiences in a revue and Nance was in Scotland for Hogmanay with relatives. On 1st January 1917 a telegram postmarked Dunoon arrived for Harry saying that John had been killed in action, and he realised that Nance had received the news first.

Mildred, broken-hearted at the death of her fiancé, came to comfort the bereaved and inconsolable father until Nance's return from Scotland. The family were shattered but managed to carry on their everyday lives. In true theatrical tradition Lauder continued with the revue, and worked hard raising money for war charities, while Nance immersed herself in hospital work. He was given permission by the War Office to entertain Scottish troops at the Front wherever they were, and he was seldom away from the firing lines, giving as many as half a dozen concerts a day.

Until John was killed, Harry and Nance had loved Glenbranter as a really wild and bonny retreat from the hassle of London life, but their son's death had knocked all their schemes and dreams on the head. In his autobiography Lauder wrote:

> One spot we fondly loved in spite of the shattering of all our hopes. It was a beautiful knoll on the north side of the main road from Dunoon to Strachur. From its summit we could look right across the glen to the two houses and the vista, no matter whether the sun smiled or the Highland mist was hanging low over the hills, always made a strong appeal to my wife and me. Here we resolved would be set up a monument to John's memory, and in due time a simple but striking monolith crowned the top of the grassy knoll. Inside the iron railing surrounding John's memorial was sufficient room for a grave on either side. One for Nance and the other for myself.

In 1919 Harry was in Australia when a telegram arrived on 1st March telling him that he was to receive a knighthood. What an accolade for a man, who started from such humble beginnings, to be the first popular Scottish artiste to be so honoured.

Although the Lauders kept their home in Dunoon they sold Glenbranter in 1921 to the Forestry Commission and bought a house in London to make life easier for Harry, who was as busy as ever. During the following years the comedian made a great deal of money and, as people do today, wisely invested in property. He bought several houses which he subsequently let. One was the Anchorage in Ardnadam (now a hotel and restaurant) and another, The Moorings in Hunter's Quay.

Helen Boyd (Nellie Watson in those days) had unique memories of the famous man and his wife, for in 1924 she entered the Lauder household as their cook.

"Sir Harry liked very plain food," Helen recalled. "And his favourite dish was roast chicken, though he was equally fond of roast beef or stewed steak or mince. Of course, he was very pleased with a meal of fresh trout that he had caught himself."

Helen had vivid memories of theatrical folk like Tommy Lorne and Tommy Morgan coming to the house. "Tommy Lorne was a great tall man and a marvellous comedian. He used to come into the kitchen and joke away with me. Lauderdale was a lovely house, full of beautiful furniture and silver, and numerous mementoes of Sir Harry's various tours abroad."

Lauderdale, with its white façade, was always a point of interest for anyone visiting Dunoon and the house was frequently brought to the notice of visitors seeing the coastline from the water. One of these was R. Morrison who recalled Mr Sands' boating station at West Bay. "Mr Sands ran a motor-boat cruise and when they passed Lauderdale there was Sir Harry walking in his garden, and as they passed he would always wave a cheery greeting to those on board."

David Beveridge remembered, "Sir Harry displayed the Union Jack upside down on a flagpole in his garden for a whole summer, despite many angry letters from local retired sea captains like myself who pointed out that it was a distress signal."

In the early 1930s Sir Harry and Tommy Lorne, with a number of other variety stars, went to Rothesay to entertain fishermen as a way of thanking them for their generosity in providing free herrings to the unemployed in Glasgow. Before the concert the artistes were entertained to lunch by the local Business Club. Sir Harry, in the course of a few remarks, said he was so little acquainted with Rothesay that he did not know there was such a thing as a Business Club. "If Rothesay had been a place like Dunoon I would have," he said. A voice from the back called out, "Where is Dunoon?"

"When you sail doon the watter," retorted Sir Harry, "you always look the wrong way. On every steamship that goes up and down the Clyde people point and say, 'There's Dunoon, that's Harry Lauder's house.' "

In April 1934 Sir Harry left Dunoon to retire to Lauder Ha', the house he had built at Strathaven, a typical little Lanarkshire town on the river Avon.

Harry Lauder died on 26th February 1950. Although he had wished to be buried next to his wife at the knoll near Glenbranter, he was laid to rest in Hamilton, the town in which he had spent so much of his youth.

At Ardentinny, by Loch Long, which is immortalised by a song of Lauder's (and previously by Tannahill) is the Ardentinny Hotel. In 1977, its owners at the time, John and Sylvia Harris, opened the Lauder Bar where they displayed an interesting collection of Lauder memorabilia, including original manuscripts and musical scores, as well as two original records of his songs, *O'er the hill to Ar dentinny* and *Bella, the Belle of Dunoon* .

On 4th November 1977 a ward at Erskine Hospital was named The Lauder-Thomson Ward in memory of Captain John Lauder. Mildred Thomson had always cherished the memory of her twenty-two-year-old fiancé, and when she died, unmarried, in 1975 at the age of eighty-three, she left the residue of her sizeable estate to Erskine Hospital. She had come to know it well through accompanying Sir Harry on his frequent visits there and she wished to provide some lasting amenity in memory of her beloved John.

Harry Lauder propagated the image of the mean Scot despite his personal generosity. It was part of his act, and has been used since by many international comedians such as Jack Benny and Bob Hope. The Scot today tends to be offended by this Lauder-created image, as well as that of the 'Music Hall Scot'. Maybe that is why Lauder is thought of so much more highly in other countries.

One thing is certain. Mention Dunoon and immediately the image of that unique man, Harry Lauder, comes to mind.

Holy Loch
and
Hunter's Quay

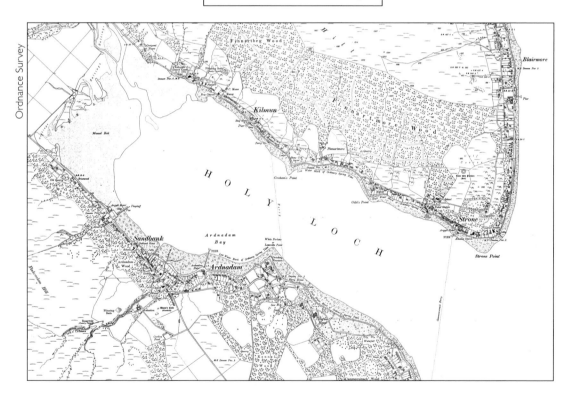

11

Holy Loch

A MILE OR SO north of Dunoon is Holy Loch, an inlet of the Firth of Clyde. At its broadest part the loch is about a mile wide and, depending on the state of the tide, between two and three miles long.

The head of the loch is particularly beautiful, surrounded by gentle sloping hills. Hugh MacDonald, the 19th-century Scottish poet and writer, was particularly fond of the hills and referred to them as 'Three mighty mountain glens.'

Nobody seems quite sure how the loch got its name. The most likely explanation is that in the sixth century St Fintan Mannu, the Irish born Celtic saint, a follower of St Columba of Iona, made his headquarters on the north shore of the loch, now Kilmun village. St Fintan Mannu is believed to have returned to Ireland to found the monastery at Teach-Mun (Tigmon) in Wexford and was Abbot there until his death in 635AD.

In 1819 a survey map of the area shows that there were very few buildings around the loch. On the Kilmun side there was the church, ancient monastery tower, the old Kilmun House, schoolhouse, inn, and a few scattered cottages. In Sandbank there was the Argyll Inn, built about 1812, and the nearest house to it was one-and-a-half miles eastward at Orchard Park, now Hafton Estate.

Apart from Sandbank, which had always been a working village, the houses round the loch were originally built as summer homes for wealthy Glasgow families. Now, most of the larger ones have been turned into flats, guest houses or hotels.

Holy Loch has always been a mecca for yachtsmen and during the summer months the loch is a venue for several regattas.

**Holy Loch in the early 1900s. The jetty
was built by a grocer in Ferguslie Street,
Sandbank, for the use of crews
victualling the numerous large yachts
moored in the loch**

539/5   Kilmun Churchyard.

Kilmun church was founded in 1442 by Sir Duncan Campbell in gratitude to the Lamonts who had allowed the burial of his son, Celestin, at Kilmun kirk. The 15th century church tower still stands beside the modern church of 1841. There is a plain square mausoleum with a domed roof on one side of the church which is the Argyll burial place for the Campbells. Among others buried in the churchyard are the shepherd, James Grieve who lived to the age of one hundred and eleven, and Elizabeth Blackwell, who in 1840 became the first woman to graduate as a doctor in the USA

12

Kilmun

ON THE SLOPES behind Kilmun village is the 180-acre Arboretum lying within the Argyll Forest Park which was established in 1935 by the Forestry Commission. Owing to the influence of the Gulf Stream, the west coast of Scotland has a mild oceanic climate enabling the Arboretum to have a fine collection of all sorts of trees and flowering shrubs as well as samples of the Dawn Redwood which, until a few years ago, was only known from fossil remains.

By the Kilmun entrance of the Arboretum can be seen old field dykes and shieling sites suggesting that the area was once grazed by Highland cattle. At some time charcoal-burners worked in the area converting elder logs into charcoal for use in iron furnaces, and also for use in the gunpowder mills at Clachaig in nearby Glen Lean.

As mentioned, Kilmun probably takes its name from St Fintan Mannu who had a cell there as early as the sixth century. This ancient village, on the north shore of the Holy Loch adjoining the small village of Strone, was given status as a Burgh in 1490 by James IV. However, Kilmun never functioned as a complete burgh although the area expanded considerably both in population and in trade. Even though Dunoon had its ancient castle, the powerful Argyll Campbells always gave Kilmun precedence.

By the goodwill of the Lamonts, the ruling clan at the time, the Campbells had the right of burial at Kilmun kirk. This privilege dated back to 1442 when Celestin, the son of Sir Duncan Campbell of Loch-awe, the Black Knight, the first of the family to assume the title of Argyll, was granted a place of burial. In gratitude Sir Duncan founded a Collegiate church for a provost and six prebendaries. The fifteenth-century church tower still stands beside the modern church of 1841.

There were early connections between the Dukes of Argyll and the Campbells of Ballochyle, for in 1658 the first Marquis granted them ferry rights extending from the Holy Loch to beyond Dunoon Castle, along some six miles of shore and across to Cloch Point. These rights were granted on condition that an ornamental eight-oared boat should always be kept ready to row the Chieftain across the Firth.

The pride of Kilmun is its church, built in 1841, and standing next to the remains of the ancient one. There is a plain square mausoleum with a domed roof on one side of the church. This is the Argyll burial place for members of the Campbell family. One whose remains lie there is Archibald, the first Marquis of Argyll (nicknamed Gillespie Grumach), the Covenant leader and Montrose's great enemy. His head was thrown into his coffin as an afterthought by warrant of Charles II, after having 'weathered' for two or three years on Edinburgh's Tollbooth Tower. The other mausoleum dates back to 1888. It was built by Charles J. Cathcart Douglas whose father, General Sir John Douglas CBE, was laid to rest there. Sir John, who built the pier at Carrick Castle, Loch Goil, had a distinguished military career and succeeded to the Glenfinart Estate in 1870. On his death in 1887 Charles inherited the estate.

In Kilmun churchyard is buried the shepherd James Grieve who died in 1911 at the unbelievable age of one hundred and eleven. Grieve, who boasted that he had smoked tobacco for a hundred years, lived at Coir-an-Tee, Loch Eck. He was said to have carried peat to the top of the hills for the bonfires that were lit to celebrate Wellington's victory over Napoleon at Waterloo in 1815.

Also buried there is Elizabeth Blackwell who in 1849 was the first woman in the world to graduate as a doctor. Elizabeth was born in Bristol in 1821, and when still a child moved with her family to the Southern States of America. She graduated with honours at Geneva College Medical School in New York State. However, once qualified, she had a long struggle to overcome social ostracism and medical prejudice to establish herself as a woman doctor.

After giving valuable service during the American Civil War, Elizabeth came to England where she had gained a great reputation, and numbered among her friends Sir James Simpson, the pioneer of the use of chloroform, and Florence Nightingale, who raised the art of nursing from a menial job to an honourable vocation.

Elizabeth discovered Kilmun in 1902 when she came for a holiday to Argyll. Maybe she came to visit Florence Nightingale whose aunt had a house in Innellan. In any case, Elizabeth fell in love with the little village and spent several happy holidays there. On her last visit she fell down the stairs of Kilmun Inn, where she was staying, and never really recovered. She soon became a complete invalid and when she received the Order of Merit shortly after her fall she was unable to comprehend the enormous honour bestowed on her.

Although she died at her English home in Hastings it was her wish to be buried in Kilmun and her remains were brought to the village in 1910.

David Napier of Kilmun who made the boiler for the engine of Henry Bell's *Comet*, Europe's first commerical steamship. Napier later pioneered iron steamships on Loch Eck

It is not possible to write about Kilmun without mentioning the inventive genius and marine engineer David Napier. David Napier was born in Dumbarton in October 1790 the son of an engineer and blacksmith. When he was twelve the family moved to Glasgow where he finished his schooling, after which he helped his father, and by the time he was twenty he was in charge of the business.

He was the first man to make and use a test tank for his ship's models and before long he designed the steamer *Rob Roy* (later bought by the French Government) which was used in 1818 on the Greenock to Belfast route carrying passengers and mail. In 1826 he engined one of the first really large passenger steamers *United Kingdom*. She was able to run her engines continuously for over twenty-four hours, an innovation at that time. The *United Kingdom* was the wonder of her day.

Two years later Napier bought land in Kilmun. At that time the village was very small indeed but the engineer saw its potential and built a stone pier, the inn, and six houses which were so alike that the locals immediately dubbed them 'the six canisters'. He then built a road from Kilmun to Loch Eck, opening up a new route to the Western Highlands. Passengers were conveyed by steam carriage to the loch where Napier had waiting for them the first of the iron steamers, the *Aglaia*.

Robert Napier, David's cousin, was equally well-known for his contribution to the Clyde's shipbuilding industry. Robert's father, like David's, was a Dumbarton blacksmith. In later years the cousins founded the well-known firm Napier and Son of Govan, Glasgow. In 1816 the families were even more closely linked together when Robert married his cousin Isabelle, David's sister. It was Robert's genius that played an important part in the introduction of steam to shipping, and his and David's combined skills did much for the Scottish shipbuilding and engineering industries.

Although resident in Glasgow, David Napier bought Glenshellish Estate between Loch Eck and Strachur, and spent his summer holidays there until he moved to London where he died, aged seventy-nine, in November 1869.

**Another Kilmun connection . . .
Captain Robert (Bob) Campbell of the famous ship-owning family of Kilmun, a much respected figure on the Clyde. This portrait appeared in the Glasgow periodical, the *Bailie***

Mitchell Library

13

Benmore

SIX MILES FROM Dunoon and north of Holy Loch in the Argyll Forest Park is situated the Estate of Benmore.

In olden days, when the property belonged to the Earls of Argyll, Benmore was simply a forest and only in later years did it become a farm with livestock. The land changed hands many times and in 1848 John Lamont, whose ancestors had owned Toward Castle, and whose family lived in Knockdow, came home from Trinidad for his annual visit. He heard that Benmore was up for sale yet again and he decided to buy the estate for his favourite nephew James, the future Laird and Baronet of Knockdow. He hoped that James, who was at that time in the Army, by owning the farm would get some valuable agricultural experience.

John Lamont engaged a Glasgow architect to build a new house to replace the existing one that was in very bad repair. As was the style favoured at the time by the wealthy, it was rather a grandiose, pretentious baronial mansion. James lived in a cottage on the estate and supervised the building of the house which, sadly, his uncle never saw, as he died before its completion.

With his uncle dead, James, who had never really found the life of a Highland Laird to his taste, sold Benmore with its new house for £17,000.

In fact, Benmore changed hands several times, and in 1870 it was sold to Mr James Duncan, a Greenock merchant who had made his fortune in sugar refining. Duncan annexed the neighbouring estate of Bernice and planted 1500 acres of coniferous woods. He also was responsible for the draining and improvements of the Echaig where he must have blasted a few strips of rock to lower the level of the river. He then enclosed and set up all the fences, many of which are still there to this day.

During the time James Duncan lived at Benmore many eminent men came to visit him. One of these was Sir Henry Morton Stanley,

Younger Botanic Garden, Benmore

The rear view of Benmore House showing its marvellous situation. John Lamont bought Benmore Estate in 1849 for his nephew James. He engaged a Glasgow architect to build a new, grandiose and rather pretentious house to replace the existing one

the journalist and explorer who made history as a reporter for the *New York Herald* when he was assigned to Africa to find the missing Scots explorer, David Livingstone. The meeting is immortalised by Stanley's casual greeting, 'Dr Livingstone, I presume'.

Another friend of James Duncan was Charles Haddon Spurgeon, the English Baptist pastor, who at twenty-two was the most popular preacher of his day. His preaching attracted vast congregations and the huge Metropolitan Tabernacle in London, seating six thousand persons, was built to cope with them.

During James Duncan's ownership of the house he built a picture gallery. He was a lover of the Arts and the gallery housed a fine collection of paintings and sculptures which, when it was open to the public, was visited by thousands of people from all over the country.

Duncan also commissioned the making of a pair of finely wrought iron gates inaccurately called 'The Golden Gates' which he exhibited at the Paris Exhibition of 1871, where they won first prize. They bear his initials, and in 1873 he had them brought back to Benmore where they were erected at the Glen Massan entrance to the estate.

Younger Botanic Garden, Benmore

The interior of the drawing room at Benmore House shows the Victorian penchant for bibelots. The atmosphere created is one of cosiness rather than grandeur

Duncan created the foundation of the magnificent gardens which can be seen today. It is often assumed that he got horticultural advice from Sir William Jackson Hooker, a director of Kew Gardens in Richmond, England, who had a summer house at Invereck (on the site of the Eventide Home) but he died in 1865, five years before Duncan had bought the estate. In all likelihood he has been confused with his son, Sir Joseph Dalton Hooker, who had also studied at Glasgow University and succeeded his father as a director at Kew.

Planted in the grounds were shrubs, flowers and a magnificent collection of trees including the avenue of towering sequoias (giant Californian conifers) which lead up to the house. The gardens contain over two hundred species of rhododendrons, making it one of the largest collections in the world, as well as many species of azalea, a vast number of exotic flowers and plants, and a unique collection of ferns. The gardens are one of the few places in the area where red squirrels can be seen.

In 1883 the estate was sold to Henry Johnston Younger, a member of the famous brewery family. During the years that he, and then his

Younger Botanic Garden, Benmore

The Conservatory and Winter Garden built in 1870 by James Duncan when he bought Benmore Estate. At one time the well-known Lady Fountain was in the Winter Garden. Puck's Hut is now on the site of the Conservatory. The Winter Glass House was ruined during a ferocious storm in the early 1920s

son, owned the property they continued to improve the gardens.

In 1928 H. G. Younger MP, gifted the gardens to the nation and today they are administered by the Royal Botanic Garden in Edinburgh. Thousands of visitors come to see them every year. The rest of the estate and the house was given to the Forestry Commission and between 1929 and 1965 the house was used as a forestry training school. In 1965 the house became the property of the Benmore Centre for Outdoor Education providing facilities for schoolchildren and adults. There are short courses in outdoor activities with instruction in orienteering, mountaineering, caving and camping. Sailing and canoeing are done on nearby Holy Loch.

Younger Botanic Garden, Benmore

The Victorian lodge keepers sitting by the Golden Gates at the Glen Massan entrance to Benmore Estate. There is nothing known about the old couple except that the man was reputed to collect and sell manure

James Duncan commissioned the making of the gates, bearing his initials, for the Paris Exhibition of 1871 where they won first prize. He brought them back in 1873 to Benmore where they still stand today

Beauty and the Beast! It is summer 1964
in the Holy Loch. Another yacht to
challenge for the America's Cup has
been built and launched from
Robertson's yard. She is *Sovreign*, seen
sailing in the vicinity of **USS** *Proteus*,
Polaris Base Depot ship.

14

Sandbank

IF YOU TAKE the High Road to Sandbank from Dunoon you will see on your left the lovely small Loch Loskin. This little loch has been greatly admired by both painters and poets and in the summer evenings can be seen a swarming mass of glow-worms.

On the hillside by the Loskin, with the old road at its back, stands Dunloskin House. On the corner stone of one of the outbuildings can be seen the Campbell crest and date 1619, for the house belonged to the Campbells of Ballochyle on condition that they supplied wine and salt to the troops of the garrison occupying Dunoon Castle.

Continuing on the High Road one reaches the village of Sandbank, formerly called Cladyhouse – house of the stony beach.

One of the oldest buildings in Sandbank was the Argyll Hotel built by Dugald McKinlay who, in the early part of the 1800s, owned numerous properties in Dunoon including the Ferry Inn. Dugald also built a distillery opposite the Argyll. Sadly the hotel was destroyed by fire in the 1980s and later demolished.

The McKinlays were a highly respected local family known for their geniality and generous hospitality. They sent their children to Dalinlongart school run by an imaginative and inspired teacher, John Taylor. Incredibly, five languages were taught at this small classless school where all the children mixed happily, no matter whether they were the laird's or the shepherd's.

One of its pupils was Dugald's third son John, who was born in Sandbank in 1819. John was a keen and studious pupil although he always preferred to be out and about in the countryside fishing and shooting and climbing the many nearby hills.

In 1835 John and his brother Alexander emigrated to Australia where their uncle, Captain McKeller, a retired shipmaster, had settled as a sheep farmer. John worked and explored beyond the settled districts of New South Wales and came to know the area very well.

In 1860 Robert O'Hara Burke was leading the first expedition (with

William Wills as his second in command) to cross Australia from Melbourne, in the south, to the Gulf of Carpentaria, in the north. The men had reached the Gulf but on their return journey no news was heard of them and it was feared that they were lost. McKinlay was in Melbourne at the time and was asked by the South Australian Government to take command of one of the four search parties looking for the explorers. John was away for nearly a year in the outback and his explorations and researches there helped greatly in the future development of the country.

John McKinlay died at Oaklands, Gawler, and a handsome monument was erected for him by his fellow colonists with the following inscription:

Erected by many Colonists as a monument to
John McKinlay a Chief amongst Australian Explorers
and Leader of the Expedition in search of
Burke and Wills 1861.
Born at Sandbank Argyllshire August 1819
Died at Oaklands 31 December 1872.

Until recent years Sandbank has always been a working village. During the Napoleonic wars there was a cooperage, employing many men and women, which supplied barrels for the gunpowder mills of Curtis & Harvey at Clachaig in Glen Lean.

The year 1876 saw the birth in the village of a small sister paper to *The Argyllshire Standard and Advertiser for the Coast* founded in 1871. Called *The Cowal Watchman* it was started by master printer William Inglis senior and was the predecessor of today's local paper the *Dunoon Observer and Ar gyllshire Standard*. William Inglis had retired from active life to Holy Loch and in 1868 had established a small printing business in Sandbank to provide employment for his large family. One of the original partners in the business was Eliza Inglis, said to be the quickest typesetter in the shop. Her grand-niece, Marion Carmichael, together with her husband John, continues the family business in John Street, Dunoon, the Sandbank premises having been demolished in 1947. In August 1996 the editorial offices and shop were totally destroyed by fire. Luckily the print works escaped the conflagration.

The year of the launch of *The Cowal Watchman* was also the year the two boatyards began business in Sandbank. These yards – Robertson & Kerr (later to be Robertson & Sons) and Morris & Lorimer – were to become famous throughout the world for their expertise in boat- and yacht-building.

Alex Robertson and Daniel Kerr were in partnership at the foundation of the firm, and when Daniel retired from the business his son,

Main Street, Sandbank   Valentine Series

(above) the main street in Sandbank in 1917. At one time Sandbank had
over twenty shops and businesses, one of which was the printing works
of *The Argyllshire Standard and Advertiser for the Coast*. The carriage is
waiting outside its premises (below left) Robert Inglis
(below right) Willie Inglis took over from his father as proprietor and
editor in 1949.

Dunoon Observer & Argyllshire Standard

93

also Daniel, remained in the yard until he retired in 1963, aged eighty-one. William Paterson, who as a young boy joined the firm in 1909, remembered vividly Mr Robertson senior, even as an old man, coming daily into the yard to see how things were going.

One of Robertson's early orders was for a fisherman in Kames. When the boat was completed she was rowed by some of the yard's men to Kames via Toward and the Kyles of Bute. Unfortunately on arrival they found the fisherman did not have the money to pay them so the men rowed the boat back to Sandbank! The following week the performance was repeated, and this time the bill was settled when they arrived at Kames. The men, having no transport, steadfastly set off on foot walking all the way home via Otter Ferry, Glendaruel, Loch Riddon, Loch Striven and Clachaig.

In those days a high capstan stood at the top of the yard near the road. This was used to pull up the heavier craft from the water's edge, which was at times a Herculean task. The form of payment was unique. When the work was finished the men would be called into the office where everyone was given a dram of whisky.

During the 1930s Robertson's was managed by three of the family, assisted by David Boyd, who was to become a big name in the world of yacht design.

In 1958 a British syndicate chose David for the coveted job of designing a challenger for the America's Cup. The last seven attempts (Thomas Lipton had tried five times and Thomas Sopwith twice) to wrest the famous Cup from its plinth in the New York Yacht Club had proved unsuccessful, and it was the fervent hope of the syndicate that at last it would come back to Britain. The yard chosen to build *Sceptre*, the British challenger, was Robertson's. This was an enormous honour, not only for the yard with its superb craftsmen, but also for Sandbank, which was to become famous for its involvement in this international competition.

Sceptre was beaten by a very fine American yacht, but she had put up such a promising performance in the race that Tony Boyden commissioned the same team to design and build *Sovreign*, the 1964 challenger. Once again the British boat was beaten and the Americans, who had held the Cup for over one hundred and thirty years, finally relinquished it to the Australians in 1983.

In 1935 the Royal National Lifeboat Institute gave Robertson's their first order. Miss Sinclair, the donor of the boat, had specifically asked for it to be built by a Scottish yard. The Duke of Montrose, head of the Scottish RNLI at the time, was at the launching of the *Charlotte Elizabeth* which was to be stationed at Port Askaig, Islay. From then on the RNLI had many of their boats built and serviced at Robertson's, until the yard went into liquidation in 1980.

Duncan Barclay

Dick Murray at work on the handsome scrollwork adorning the bow of
Sceptre, **designed by the yacht's architect, David Boyd. Dick came to
Robertson's as a lad and became foreman boatbuilder, a job he held
until he retired**

Duncan Barclay

The launch of *Sceptre* in April 1958 at Robertson's Yard,
Sandbank. A syndicate of Royal Yacht Squadron members
paid £30,000 for the 12-metre vessel to challenge for the
America's Cup. Sadly, *Sceptre* was soundly beaten
(below right) yachts on the slipway of the Morris & Lorimer
yard (below left) an aerial view of Morris & Lorimer

John Saidler

Molly McLachlan

Like Robertson's, Morris & Lorimer was to become a family firm. Robert Lorimer had been yard manager in one of the Clyde's biggest shipyards at Fairfield. On retiring to Kirn, he and a local small boatbuilder, Morris, decided to start a boatyard in Sandbank. Shortly afterwards Morris died and Lorimer's son, who at the time was in the timber business, joined the firm, as did the founder's grandson, also Robert.

Both of the Sandbank yards produced some of the world's most beautiful yachts as well as a great number of commercial and other craft. Launches, lifeboats and dinghies were needed by the large steam yachts built by the big Clyde shipyards and many of these orders, including a gig for King George V's yacht *Britannia*, came to the Holy Loch boatyards.

Molly McLachlan, whose great-grandfather founded Morris & Lorimer, worked in the office in the 1930s and remembered one day a telegram being received by the yard manager, Mr Tait. "It was to ask him to send a steward to a yacht in the South of France. Mr Tait managed to find a suitable man for the job. Leo, I think his name was. On his return from France Mr Tait asked him how he had got on. Leo replied, 'Oh, fine. As soon as I arrived I had a great poker lunch.' Mr Tait was mystified. 'What's a poker lunch?' he asked. 'Three Kings and Two Queens,' was the reply."

The other nice tale about royalty that Molly related was when the yard rigger, Euan McPhail, went to the Mediterranean for the six-metre races. Euan was on board with the Princess of Spain when the runner broke. Euan knew the mast was going to come down so he shouted at her, "Mind your heid." Startled the Princess repeated, "Heid?" But somehow Euan managed to get the message across to her just in time.

It is difficult today to visualise Holy Loch in the heyday of the boatyards. The loch was full of pleasure boats, paddle steamers, small sailing and fishing boats and, of course, those magnificent luxurious yachts owned by men connected with all the big businesses of their day: Templeton Carpets, Teacher's Whisky, Kelvin Engines, Camp Coffee, Singer Sewing Machines, to name just a few.

During the winter the yards were busy repairing and overhauling yachts and miscellaneous small boats. Usually the yacht's skipper and engineer would stay with their ship, but most of the crew would be laid off until the following season.

There were also unemployed commercial craft moored in the loch and it would be a common sight to see the Lascar crews hanging out endless lines of washing to dry in the wind.

With the coming of the Second World War, as in the First, both yards were busy executing orders from the Admiralty for all types of craft such as motor torpedo boats, launches and auxiliary vessels.

Harvester House (on the site of what was for many years a petrol station and garage) became a small naval establishment, and Sandbank was an important part of the war effort.

When the war ended boatbuilding had changed dramatically. The days of the large steam yachts, owned by the wealthy few, had gone forever and instead there was a slowly reviving market for small racing and cruising boats that could be enjoyed by the less affluent. Of course, there was still an occasional order for the large motor or sailing yacht, but generally boatyards concentrated on smaller vessels.

This also applied to the yards at Sandbank. Robertson's concentrated on building six- and twelve-metre racing boats as well as the *Loch Long* and *Piper* class boats. They, of course, still continued to build pilot boats, RNLI vessels and other similar craft, while Morris and Lorimer concentrated on commercial boats, overhauls, repairs and storage. However, at the beginning of the 1950s Robert Lorimer was in ill-health and the yard was sold to the well-known yachtsman, James Howden Hume. The US Navy demolished the yard sheds and replaced them with the one that still exists on the original site. Now a private developer uses it for storage.

In the late 1950s Colonel Whitbread, of the famous brewery firm, commissioned Robertson's to build one of their most beautiful yachts, *Lone Fox*, designed by Robert Clark, the creator of *Gipsy Moth V* for Sir Francis Chichester.

In the 1960s the industry faced an enormous change in its boat construction with the development of a new material – glass reinforced plastic. This caused the boat market to expand in a way hitherto unimagined. Robertson's began to fit out glass-fibre hulls, and in the mid-1970s built special workshops for GRP construction.

In 1966 the Robertson family sold the firm to an investment company but many of the long-serving men like James Bruce, William Cameron, Malcolm (Calum) McLachlan, William Ponton and Alexander McQueen stayed on until the firm went into liquidation.

Part of the premises were taken over by Terry Hooper. When he left in 1993, the sheds on the shore side of the yard, as well as the pier, were demolished.

15

Ardnadam

ARDNADAM IS A continuation of Sandbank and is now mostly residential. In 1867, however, there was a small joiners and builders business owned by John Taylor from Peebleshire behind his villa Ardendarroch, now called Fairholm.

Ardnadam has a pier, the longest on the Clyde, which is still in reasonable repair as it was used by the US Navy attached to the Polaris Submarine Base. The Navy also used the now demolished Ardnadam Hotel as their Shore Support Base.

The origin of the name most likely comes from the prehistoric pagan altar which stands on the hillside above the pier. As in medieval churches, these places were also used for the burial of the dead, hence the name *Ard-na-Tuam* – the height of the grave.

Along the shore road in the direction of Dunoon is Lazaretto Point (called White Farlane on Admiralty charts) with its tall tower, a war memorial to the dead of both World Wars. Of particular interest is the inscription commemorating the death of the crews of six submarines who sailed from Holy Loch, never to return.

The point takes its name from the quarantine station with its extensive range of storage houses which was built in 1807 during the Napoleonic Wars. Lazar House, or Lazaretto, was the name for a hospital, first established by the Order of St Lazarus, which looked after persons suffering from leprosy, the plague and other infectious and contagious diseases. Ships from foreign ports would ride out the period of quarantine, while their cargo would be discharged on to the station, exposing it to the purifying influence of the air. Any contagious or infectious crew were also put ashore.

In the grounds of the demolished house Ros-Mhor (once the home of George Outram, owner of *The Herald*) is the original lookout tower for the quarantine station. The Fir Park Hotel and houses round the point, up to and including Woodglen, have the original wall at the back of their gardens. Glen Cottage, next to Woodglen, is the old customs

An artist's impression of Holy Loch shows the quarantine station opposite Kilmun. Built in 1807 during the Napoleonic Wars, ships' crews thought to be infectious would serve their quarantine period there

house, built in the early 1800s. Marjorie Smith, who lived in Beneli, told me that at the back of her house there was a hole in the wall through which kind folk used to push food and drink to the quarantined inmates.

Because of the hold-up at the quarantine station there was considerable delay to Clyde shipping, so the government decided to abandon the scheme, and in 1840 the buildings were pulled down, the site cleared and the land feud.

Alexander Waddell, a man of many talents, owned the now demolished Ferry Cottage at Ardnadam. Since 1840 the ferry rights, dating back to Bonnie Prince Charlie's time, had been in his family. Alex's father came from Glen Lean and his Uncle Alex, after whom he was named, was piermaster. He also owned a contracting business which at that time was run with carts and horses. Alex's father used to ferry people across Holy Loch to and from Miriam's Point at Kilmun. This was a very busy crossing, for although the steamers called at piers around the loch, they did not have a direct service across it. The owners of Hafton Estate objected to all the folk coming and going across their private estate (at that time their land went right to the water's edge) so the small lane at the side of the ferry house was built.

Alex had memories of the Sandbank road being an earthen farm

The ferryman's cottage, Ardnadam will always be associated with the Waddell family who, from 1840, had the ferry rights from Lazaretto Point to Kilmun

Eileen Lea

Ferryman Alex Waddell on the Holy Loch

track from Lazaretto right along to Hunter's Quay before it was made into a road in the early 1920s, just before the Allan family bought Hafton Estate.

Alec also remembered the horse-drawn brake which he used regularly when he went to and from Sandbank as a small boy. One did not pay for it, as there was a big step at the back and the boys used to sit up there and get a free ride. Peter MacFarlane shared this memory: "Four persons sat each side of the brake and one or two beside the driver. Behind there was a small door and a step on a bracket. Small boys tried to steal rides on this and pedestrians would call out 'whip behind'. It was a very pleasant form of transport although somewhat cramped and, of course, there was no protection from the weather though passengers with umbrellas used them when it rained.

"The drivers came in for a certain amount of tormenting from us small boys. I remember two on one bicycle following a brake. One rode the bike while the other sat precariously on the handlebars and armed with a pea-shooter peppered the cabby. The driver stopped and shouted threats, making menacing gestures with his whip. The cyclist stopped at a safe distance, but an elderly gentleman out walking, crossed the road waving his walking stick, and obviously by his gestures put the tormentors to flight."

Hafton Holiday Lodges Ltd

Hafton House is set in beautiful parkland which was once part of a 140-acre estate. James Hunter bought the property in 1816 and asked the well-known architect, David Hamilton to redesign the then existing house.
In about 1840 substantial additions were made. Built in the Gothic style, a replication of Renaissance architecture adopted in most European countries, Hafton House is an impressive edifice

16

Hafton

A SHORT WAY from Lazaretto Point is the impressive and lovely Hafton Estate. Today, the 140-acre estate of beautiful parkland, with breath-taking seascapes that once belonged to one family, accommodates two large holiday developments – the Hafton Holiday Centre consisting of self-catering holiday lodges and a leisure centre, and the Holy Loch Holiday Park.

At the end of the eighteenth century John Lamont and his brother Neil became partners in the tenancy of part of Hafton Estate which was owned by the Campbells of Ballochyle. John was the paternal great-grandfather of Colonel Daniel Lamont who, in the 1890s, was a Secretary for War in the United States.

The brothers were happy, contented and industrious tenants and lived in peace until 1802 when they were cruelly evicted from their home. The trouble was that they had become Baptists through hearing the preaching of an Evangelist, Donald MacArthur. The clergy of the established church were very jealous and resentful of MacArthur's popularity and success and began to persecute him and his followers, whom they denounced as heretics and disturbers of the peace.

A petition against the Lamonts was drawn up by Campbell of Southall and signed by all the Lairds of the district except Lamont of Knockdow, who refused to lift a finger against his two kinsmen.

A few years later, in 1816, James Hunter bought Hafton Estate and its small mansion house, known as Orchard Park from the Camp-bells of Ballochyle. Hunter asked David Hamilton to redesign the house for him and once again the architect produced a baronial type of mansion so popular at the time. Hunter foresaw the enormous potential of steam and knew that it would open up the Clyde coast to visitors and landowners, so in 1828 he built a sturdy pier, not far from his estate, which he named Hunter's Quay. It is the name now given to the district between Ardnadam and Kirn.

James Hunter together with James Ewing and Kirkman Finlay

copyright RCAHMS

Hafton House's 1840 additions included the interior pointed arch, dominant feature of Gothic architecture, as commonly seen in cathedrals and churches

The exquisite design and tracery in the domed ceiling verges towards flamboyancy, a characteristic not uncommon among Scottish architects of the time

copyright RCAHMS

were, without doubt, the founders of Dunoon's prosperity.

In the mid-1880s, as a young boy, General Sir Ian Hamilton lived at Hafton. Owing to his mother's death when he was three years old, Hamilton had been brought up on the estate which was rented by his grandparents. There he learned to shoot and developed an eye for the countryside and country pursuits. In those days there was an enormous variety of animal and bird life at Hafton. Roaming on the land were otters, red deer, badgers, stoats and weasels as well as plovers, curlews, sparrow-hawks and kestrels. There was no shortage of game either, and offshore shellfish was plentiful, for Hunter had laid down oyster and mussel beds during his ownership.

General Sir Ian Hamilton returned to the area in 1923 and on the 27th January unveiled the war memorial opposite the pier at Dunoon.

At that time the estate was in the hands of the Allan family of the famous shipping line. Alexander Allan was a doctor of literature and had three daughters. Isabella Mac-Vicar remembered them well: "The Allans were great benefactors to the district. The girls were good skiers and skaters as well as being extremely fond of yachting." Isabella also recalled the great parties held at Hafton at Christmas. "There was always a big Christmas tree and a gift for everyone. You were asked beforehand to make a list of what you would like and you usually received it."

Alex Waddell, too, remembered the Allan's generosity: "Apart from being involved with the Girl Guides and the elderly, the Allan sisters built a recreational centre in Sandbank." When the surviving daughter Elspeth died, the house and estate lay neglected until it was sold in 1980.

T & R Annan

PS *Caledonia* at Hunter's Quay in 1899.
The pier was built in 1858 replacing a
stone one which had been erected in
1828 by James Hunter of Hafton Estate.
In 1969 it was bought by Western
Ferries and was opened on 3rd June that
year as another link between Dunoon
and Gourock. The *Caledonia* was a
medium-sized steamer elegantly fitted
out for her passengers

(above) *Vigilant* and *Britannia* racing on the Clyde in the 1890s. Racing yachts had richly furnished and decorated saloons in which their owners exchanged hospitality

(below left) Royal Clyde Yacht Club House at Hunter's Quay around 1900, now the Royal Marine Hotel

(below right) The old telegraph office at Hunter's Quay now a sub-post office and newsagents by Western Ferries' terminal

17

Halcyon Days

CAMMERSREINACH – THE BAY of ferns – was the original name of Hunter's Quay and was a busy ferry point for crossing the Firth. There is a road leading up the hill opposite the pier that still bears that name.

Hunter's Quay is now the headquarters of Western Ferries which operates a car ferry service to McInroy's Point, just outside Gourock.

L. D. Henderson, grandson of the founder of the famous Glasgow shipbuilders at Meadowside, Partick, writing in 1935 of his childhood, described the Cowal shore. The family had a house by Hunter's Quay where they spent twelve consecutive summers. "The shore was then a haven of peace, the only public conveyances which raised the dust of the often very dusty shore road were the imposing five-horse coaches which carried tourists by the shores of Loch Eck to Strachur in connection with the *Lord of the Isles* tour. Sometimes there would be three in procession with their red-coated drivers in white beaver top-hats and similarly dressed guards with post-horns, their outward journey in the morning and their afternoon return, to the tootling of the post-horns which provided the most thrilling events of an otherwise tranquil day except, of course, for Regatta days."

Mary Fraser reckoned she had lived longer on the Shore Road than any other resident in Hunter's Quay. Mary particularly had memories of an elderly couple called King who lived in Dunivard. Mr King had connections with Alexander Graham Bell, the inventor of the telephone. This must be the house that Donald Macdonald recalled visiting in the 1950s which had the remnants of an internal and complicated telephone system installation.

At one time Hunter's Quay was synonymous with yacht Regattas and was a name in the yachting world matching that of Cowes on the Isle of Wight.

Hunter's Quay arrived on the yachting map comparatively late and in a small way. Apart from the prestigious Royal Yacht Squadron at Cowes, organised club yacht racing was already taking place in

Ireland, on the Dee, the Thames and at Plymouth. In Scotland, 1824 saw the establishment of the Northern Yacht Club at Rothesay, and the Club attained the 'Royal' prefix six years later. This Club was holding Regattas off Dunoon in the 1830s, including a race for the 'Dunoon Cup'.

Because the Club put a size limitation on members' boats of not less than 8 tons, the Clyde Model Yacht Club was founded in September 1856 for less well-endowed sailing enthusiasts. By 1864 the word 'Model' was dropped, the membership expanded to include larger boats, and in 1861 it became the Clyde Yacht Club. Ten years later it received the Queen's permission to use the prefix 'Royal'. At that time Mr Hunter of Hafton was building a private hotel at Hunter's Quay and agreed to let off a few rooms for the exclusive use of the Club. Some years later the Club bought the hotel (later to become the Royal Marine Hotel) from Hunter for £4,200.

In 1873 the exclusive Mudhook Yacht Club was founded for the purpose of promoting amateur seamanship amongst yachtsmen. The Club was so unique that it called its chief flag officer 'Admiral' instead of the usual 'Commodore'. As the Club did not have its own premises it was invited to use those of the Royal Clyde Yacht Club.

L. D. Henderson in 1935 recalled: "As a boy I knew all the five original members of the famous Mudhook Club. Having been friends for more than thirty years with the Admiral, James Reid, I heard many tales of the early skylarking that went on well into the second decade of the Mudhook's existence. At that time the Firth was not the busy estuary it is today and the yachting fraternity was a small and exclusive circle.

"Naturally, there was a personal friendliness amongst them which tolerated much practical joking and leg-pulling that would probably be taken in ill part today. I can imagine the modern young yachtsman, whose dinghy had been missing for a few days, not quite appreciating the joke if it happened to be delivered by a railway lorry at his Buchanan Street office door in Glasgow with carriage to pay."

The Royal Clyde Yacht Club felt that it 'had arrived' when, in 1876, Queen Victoria presented it with a very handsome, elegant and valuable cup to be given as a prize during the racing season.

Two years later in July a disaster occurred. There was a serious fire at the hotel which luckily started during the day, so no one was hurt. However, no time was wasted in rebuilding and the new hotel, which was the Club House as well as being open to members' guests, was one of the best examples of the half-timber style of architecture in Scotland. The house was designed by T. L. Watson, a cousin of the famous naval architect George Lennox Watson.

The housewarming took place in 1890 and for the dinners of that opening season one was asked to wear morning dress. The bay beyond the jetty for that season was so crowded with yachts that in the words of one contemporary writer, "It looked from the shore as though you could cross dryshod from the slip at Cammesreinach to Strone Point."

Members used to arrive at Hunter's Quay by steamer on a Friday or Saturday, staying for a leisurely weekend. The Club House was the most important place in the neighbourhood and, in fact, it was owing to the Club's initiative that a telegraph office was opened in 1888 opposite the pier. This still survives today as a minute sub-post office and newsagent. It was a busy place during Regatta weeks, and young boys made quite a bit of pocket-money rowing dinghies between the moored yachts to hand out recently delivered telegrams.

In 1893 yachting reached its peak when both the Prince of Wales and Lord Dunraven went to G. L. Watson for the designs of two of the finest yachts ever built – *Britannia* and *Valkyrie II* both built by D. W. Henderson of Meadowside on the Clyde.

The summer of 1894 was a great year for the Royal Clyde Yacht Club despite the tragedy which marked the start of the race for the Muir Memorial Challenge Cup. There was a collision between *Satanita* and *Valkyrie*, the latter sinking off Hunter's Quay with the death of one crew member. The Prince of Wales's *Britannia* won many races, and so many yachts came for Clyde Fortnight that the Holy Loch was unable to accommodate them so that they had to find safe anchorages on the other side of the Firth from Gourock to Rothesay.

In 1902 the Club made formal application for the patronage of the new King, Edward VII. At that time the Club had a membership of over one thousand, with four hundred yachts sporting its burgee. The list of its members read like *Who's Who*, for apart from aristocracy, the cream of Glasgow's businessmen were among its members.

The Clyde was also becoming a great centre for yacht-building having produced three of the world's most distinguished yacht designers – William Fife the second, George Lennox Watson, the designer of *Britannia*, and Alfred Mylne. These remarkable men and their influence took the Club to a leading place in the world of international yachting. All three had been trained in shipbuilding yards and designed some of the greatest racing yachts of the period.

Clyde Fortnight was so important a date in the diaries of the rich yachting fraternity that in 1900 the Royal Clyde Yacht Club made 'representations' to the German Kaiser, firmly pointing out that the dates he had fixed for Kiel Regatta would conflict with those already fixed for Clyde Fortnight. The German Emperor changed his dates!

It is ironic that one of the staunch pillars of the Royal Clyde Yacht Club, Walter Bergius, produced his Kelvin engine and thereby started a revolution. His early engines started on petrol and ran on paraffin, and were to have an enormous influence on both the small man's cruising habits and on the inshore fishing industry which hitherto worked under sail.

Up to the First World War Clyde Fortnight was an annual success, and even in 1914 there were yachts racing such as *Britannia, Wendur, Rose* and *Adela*, but it must be noted that the royal yacht withdrew from the last few races because of the gravity of the situation.

Clyde Fortnight was resumed in 1919, a year after the end of hostilities. That year the Club had to find a new Commodore as Lord Inverclyde of the Cunard Steamship Company, who had held the office for thirty years, had died. Before his death he had, however, enjoyed the whole fortnight on his steam-yacht *Beryl* on which a frequent visitor was Haile Selassie, the Emperor of Ethiopia. Lord Inverclyde was succeeded by another man connected with Cunard, Sir Charles McIver. Although Sir Charles was not a Scot, he had close associations with the Club and with the Clyde. He had been an active member of the Club since 1892 and was the son of David McIver, one of the wealthiest and keenest yachtsmen of his day whose handsome yacht *Brenda* carried off the first championship the Club ever organised in 1858.

The first time that a reigning monarch came to the Clyde to join in the racing was in 1920. *Britannia*, refitted only the year before, arrived at Hunter's Quay in June, towed up from Cowes by a destroyer, to be greeted with wild enthusiasm and excitement. In July she was joined by King George V, and during the Fortnight *Britannia* was racing with a fair amount of success with Major Sir Philip Hunloke at the helm. Sir Philip was the King's sailing master and an amateur helmsman widely respected among the professional skippers.

Britannia was to become the world's most raced and successful yacht, winning her hundredth race on 6th August 1930. Her notable career lasted until the death of King George V in 1936. The King had always wanted the ship to remain in his hands, and he hated the thought of her becoming neglected and derelict. So with depth charges placed in her bilges she was towed by two destroyers into the middle of the English Channel and blown up.

Towards the end of the 1920s and during the 1930s a new class of racing yachts with modern rig was built, not quite so large as those of the Victorian era. This was the stunningly beautiful 'J' Class. These boats were generally regarded as the height of extravagance in pleasure sailing and sadly were a short-lived class owing to the expense of their upkeep and amount of crew needed to race them. Many came up to the Clyde and some of the most memorable ones were *Shamrock V, Velsheda* and *Endeavour I* and *II*.

The Royal Clyde Yacht Club prospered until the depression of the early 1930s when Clyde Fortnight was suspended for two years. But soon things picked up and the Firth once again was the scene of fine racing yachts with colourful owners and crews.

The thirties came to a close and once again the continuity of the Club was broken by the outbreak of war. Alex Waddell remembered 3rd September 1939, the day war was declared. "I was out there on the starting line. We used to take down the racing marks for the flag-boats and that day there was a conference going on in the stern of the Committee vessel as to whether the race was to be cancelled and the flag marks taken away. Imagine, they got as far as the third mark before cancelling anything."

At the close of hostilities in 1945 the yachting scene had changed for ever. Individual wealth had greatly diminished and it was no longer possible to run big yachts with large crews. At last yachting was becoming geared to the average man and his family. Clyde Fortnight was reduced to a week and finally to a weekend with the venue being at one of the major Clyde resorts.

During the 1950s and 1960s the Clyde scene was greatly enhanced by the very competitive International Dragon Class yachts, small boats which provided a brilliant spectacle with their infinite array of hull and spinnaker colours, and the Dragon Gold Cup brought boats and helmsmen to the Clyde from all over Europe.

One cannot write about the Royal Clyde Yacht Club without mentioning one of its most colourful members – Sir Thomas Lipton.

Lipton was born in 1850, the son of a poor Irish labourer who left his native country because of the potato famine. He moved to Glasgow where he eventually opened a small grocer's shop. At the age of nine, his son, Thomas, started working in the shop as an errand boy and then a year or two later moved on to a shirt shop where he earned four shillings a week. At fifteen, the lad sailed for America with thirty shillings in his pocket, and without knowing anyone. He worked on tobacco plantations in Virginia and rice fields in South Carolina, and then stowed away in a ship bound for New York where he managed to find a job in a big grocer's shop. However, he became homesick and returned to Glasgow when he was twenty.

In one year he managed to save £100 and on his twenty-first birthday he opened his own shop. At thirty years of age the errand boy had become a millionaire.

Thomas Lipton then expanded his business and bought tea plantations in Ceylon, thereby ensuring his shops' supplies. Then all his energy was thrown into building up his various businesses. After 1897 he started his great charity work which brought him a knighthood and a baronetcy in 1902.

It was in his steam yacht, *Erin* that the former lad, who had left

Mitchell Library

Sir Thomas Lipton at the wheel of *Shamrock IV*. Lipton owned five Shamrocks which he named after Shamrock Green Mills near Clones Co Monaghan, where his father had worked as a poor labourer before emigrating to Scotland. The wheel of *Shamrock III* has been loaned to the Dunoon & Cowal Heritage Society and can be seen in Caste House Museum

(below) the interior saloon of *Erin was comparable with the most sumptious drawing rooms of the era*

school at nine years of age, entertained King Edward VII, as well as many other distinguished and high-ranking persons. Though Sir Thomas was a teetotaller, he was a lavish and genial host and was noted for his splendid hospitality and perpetual good humour.

Sir Thomas was an unsuccessful challenger for the America's Cup, having tried to win it back five times with his five green-hulled yachts all named *Shamrock*. Although he never won the coveted Cup, he earned from the Americans the reputation of being the world's best loser, and after his last challenge in 1930 the New York Yacht Club presented him with a gold cup and an album of members' signatures in appreciation of his sportsmanship.

Sir Thomas's adviser in yachting matters was Colonel Duncan Neill, a scion of one of the great Greenock sugar-refining dynasties, all members being keen yachtsmen. It was Neill who was usually at the helm during a race.

Sir Thomas, affectionately known as 'Tommy', died in 1931 leaving most of his fortune to Glasgow charities.

Innellan and Toward

When Innellan pier was erected in 1850 more people built villas, and the village became a popular Clydeside resort.
In 1900 the pier had to be extended as the new steamers with their deeper draught could not get in at low water. The PS *Waverley* was the last steamer to call at Innellan pier in 1972. Although it was reopened briefly in 1974 to take oil rig workers to the yard at Ardyne, the pier is now derelict

18

Early Days

A holiday in a quiet spot
Watching the ships.
There is a pleasure in the pathless woods,
There is a rapture on the lonely shore.
There is society where none intrudes
By the deep sea, and music in its road.

THESE LINES WRITTEN after a visit by the romantic nineteenth-century poet, Lord Byron, reflect the charm of Innellan, the small village four miles south of Dunoon on the road to Toward.

As with other place names, no one is quite certain about the origin of Innellan. Most consider that the name derives from *Eun-eilean*, Gaelic for bird island, as there is offshore a haven for birds called Perch Island. Seventy-one-year-old Allan Park Paton in 1889 made people reconsider this theory. In 1843 Paton was a solicitor and former agent and factor for the Ineland estate (as Innellan was then called). He wrote a letter on the back of an old estate plan of the village foreshore stating that it was he who had changed the name from Ineland, pronounced *In-land*, to Innellan, as he could not find a more unsuitable name than In-land for a watering place.

Although the Campbells of Auchenbrack in 1650 built Knocka-millie Castle on the hill behind Innellan, a few ruins of which remain, Innellan only became of any significance in the middle of the last century when, like other towns and villages on the Clyde, it was discovered by Glaswegians and other city dwellers as the perfect place for a summer holiday. It became a popular and smart holiday resort, and men with money to spare built sumptuous summer villas for their families in the lovely peaceful village with its unspoilt hinterland rich in flora, fauna and birdlife.

This stretch of the Clyde is broad and open, and the views from

Innellan's Royal Hotel was a very fashionable venue. It had a beautiful staircase down which many a radiant bride descended. Sadly, it was another of Cowal's impressive buildings to have burned down

ROYAL HOTEL, INNELLAN, ARGYLL.

Innellan are marvellous, encompassing on the opposite shore Skelmorlie and the Ayrshire coast and to the south the hills of Bute, the isles of Cumbrae and, on a clear day, Arran and Ailsa Craig, that solid rock set in the middle of the sea.

Before Innellan pier and waiting rooms were built in 1851, great dependence was put on the ferryman. There is a story that a ferryman from the opposite side of the Firth was asked by the local minister to take him across on a day when there was a hard east wind blowing. He refused saying, "If we're drowned it would be easy to get another minister, but it would be very difficult to get another ferryman." In those days the ferryman usually dropped the passengers from the big boats opposite their homes, but it was often a rather dangerous business. The ferry house was also a licensed public house, and passengers transported by the ferryman were given a small sixpenny ticket, which included a bottle of ale at the inn.

1864 saw the opening of the Wemyss Bay Railway with its steamer connection, and this service increased Innellan's popularity as a resort.

One of the first houses to be built in Innellan, shortly after it became a popular holiday place, was Craigie Michael. Built by a Mr Cooke for his family, it became a regular summer holiday home for Florence Nightingale, the legendary 'Lady of the Lamp'. In 1854 wealthy-born Florence Nightingale, during the height of the Crimean War, took a staff of nurses to run the hospital at Scutari, Turkey. Within six months of being there she had reduced the death rate for British soldiers from 42% to 2%. It is thanks to this remarkable woman that there is a nurses' training school at the famous London teaching hospital, St Thomas's.

One of the many prominent persons of the time to have a summer home in Innellan was the Scottish thread manufacturer of Paisley, Sir Peter Coats. The Scots theologian and botanist, Henry Drummond (1851-1897), Professor of Natural Science at Glasgow's Free Church College, was a frequent visitor to the watering-place, as were Lord and Lady Aberdeen. Lord Aberdeen was twice Viceroy of Ireland, and in 1893 became, for a period of five years, Governor-General of Canada. Lady Aberdeen, the youngest daughter of the first Lord Tweedmouth, was a personality in her own right and was very interested in women's questions of her day.

John Ross, amateur champion sculler of Great Britain in the 1870s, and later world champion, came with his family from Greenock to settle in Innellan. One of David Napier's foreman blacksmiths, Arthur Fordyce, retired to the village in about 1870. An Edinburgh man, he named his house after the prominent hill in that city, Arthur's Seat. Fordyce could not bear giving up work so he set up a small smithy near his home, and horsemen and farmers came from all over the area to have their horses shod. It was said that there was nothing that Arthur could not make or mend. He invented tree-pruning shears which had a cutting blade with eccentric action. Fordyce also made a small steam engine which used to run round his dining-table much to the interest of visitors and to the fascination of the local children.

In the late 1920s and 1930s Robert (Bob) Hay lived at Churnside, just outside Innellan. Hay's eldest son, also Robert, spent most of his holidays there. In later years he became the last Director-General of the Indian Medical Services and as such was responsible in 1947 for handing over the medical services to the newly formed Indian Government. At that time he was made a Knight Commander of the Indian Empire and became Honorary Physician to King George VI.

Innellan will always be associated with the Rev Dr George Matheson who was for eighteen years Minister of the Parish Church. George Matheson was born on 27th March 1842, the eldest son of a family of five children whose father was a respected and successful Glasgow merchant. When he was a child, George's sight was impaired, and by the time he was eighteen he was blind. Despite this handicap he took his MA with honours and in 1874 became a Doctor of Divinity. Besides being a clergyman he was also a poet, writer and philosopher.

A tall man with a spare frame, George had a ruddy pleasant countenance and, although blind, his eyes were penetrating. He was a born optimist, always enjoying life to the full. A witty and humorous man, he had a cheerful and buoyant disposition which made everyone he met feel immediately at ease in his company. Matheson was a born actor and wonderful mimic, entertaining his friends for hours on end with his varied gifts.

It was in April 1869 that Matheson became minister of Innellan's

Rev Dr George Matheson (1842 – 1905) was the blind minister at Innellan's Parish Church for eighteen years. During this time he wrote many religious books and a great deal of sacred poetry. In 1882 he composed what was to become his most famous hymn, *O Love that Wilt Not Let Me Go*. Gifted with an excellent memory, Matheson preached marvellously inspiring sermons to a filled Parish Church Sunday after Sunday

Mitchell Library

Chapel of Ease, and in 1870 the chapel became the Parish Church of Innellan.

George Matheson was not just a superb orator but also an extremely caring pastor. He took his duties very seriously and was a great comfort to all who came into contact with him.

Despite being blind the preacher loved to travel on the Clyde steamers and became a well-known and much loved figure to the captains and crews.

At that time it was the ambition of most Church of Scotland ministers to preach before Queen Victoria at Balmoral. The usual procedure was for a list to be submitted to the Queen for her approval but sometimes she, herself, put forward the name of a man she particularly wanted to meet. Thus George Matheson came to preach at Balmoral in October 1885.

A bachelor, George Matheson was greatly helped in his life by the devotion of his sister, who looked after him faithfully and affectionately throughout his lifetime. As he said shortly before he died, his happy life was largely due to the enormous contribution she had made towards his welfare.

Matheson was sixty-four when he died at North Berwick on 28th August 1906, and he was buried in the family vault in Glasgow's Necropolis. He will always be remembered as an exceptional minister, writer and poet and as 'Matheson of Innellan'.

T & R Annan

Mitchell Library

(above) Castle Toward is often confused with Toward Castle, the Lamont stronghold of days gone by. Castle Toward was designed by David Hamilton in about 1819 for Glasgow merchant, Kirkman Finlay. It is a typically large, pretentious, baronial mansion so loved by wealthy Glaswegians in the eighteenth and nineteenth centuries. Today Castle Toward is an Outdoor Education Centre and hosts business and social events

(left) Kirkman Finlay was one of Glasgow's most prominent merchants. At the age of eighteen he ran the successful family cotton export business. He was Glasgow's Lord Provost in 1812 and 1819. He was an influential figure in the growth of Dunoon and died at Castle Toward in 1842

19

Days Gone By

TWO MILES SOUTH of Innellan is the small clachan of Toward. Its well-known headland, Toward Point, is a celebrated navigational mark for shipping, with its fifty-six foot tall lighthouse built in 1812.

Toward has always been associated with the Lamonts for they were, for a long time, the ruling clan of Cowal. There were always feuds between the Lamonts and the Campbells, the rival clan of the area, and these culminated tragically in the terrible massacre of 1646. Toward Castle, the Lamont stronghold at that time, is now a mass of ruins. People often confuse this castle with Castle Toward. The latter is another of those large, pretentious, baronial mansions so loved by the wealthy men of Glasgow during the late eighteenth and early nineteenth centuries. As so many other buildings in the Cowal District, this house was designed, in about 1819, by David Hamilton for Kirkman Finlay.

Finlay was one of the outstanding entrepreneurs of nineteenth-century Glasgow. During the Napoleonic War Finlay, with his fleet of fast ships manned by experienced crews, did much to break Napoleon's blockade, which was intended to starve Britain into submission. He also established in Glasgow the production of cotton, which had previously been confined to the manufacturing mills of industrial England. Kirkman Finlay contributed a great deal to the prosperity of Glasgow and the city recognised his worth, electing him its MP in 1812, and seven years later making him Rector of the University, and at one period its Lord Provost.

During his ownership of Castle Toward Finlay planted at least five million trees over nine hundred acres of land. He also enclosed, drained and tilled the fields of the estate making it a model of farming methods which were admired and copied throughout the area.

A frequent visitor to Castle Toward was the future Liberal Prime Minister, William Gladstone. Gladstone's name is on the subscription list of Holy Trinity Church, Dunoon, where he used to worship when visiting his friend Kirkman Finlay.

Kirkman died in 1842 and his son, Alexander Struthers Finlay, a JP, and later MP for Argyll, inherited the property.

Descendants of Kirkman Finlay still owned the house in the days of Isabella MacVicar's childhood. She remembered, "They had an Argyll motor-car with a klaxon horn. It was simply wonderful. Whenever I heard the klaxon I would say to myself 'Castle Toward'." Isabella recalled some of the Coats family (the famous thread manufacturers of Paisley) living there in the 1930s, during the summer months. A huge station wagon used to pick them up from Dunoon pier, where they arrived with piles of luggage and an assortment of dogs.

Today, Castle Toward is an Outdoor Education Centre run by a Trust. It also acts as a venue for business meetings, corporate training and social functions.

Down Memory Lane

Dunoon Grammar School

Happy Dunoon Grammar School teachers on an outing in the 1920s. Thirty years later the school in Hillfoot Street was severely damaged by fire and it was decided that the Primary and Secondary classes should be split and that the latter should have their own building. On 13th March 1964 the new Secondary School at Ardenslate Road was formally opened by the Secretary of State for Scotland, the Rt Hon Michael Noble MP

20

Schooldays

IN 1641 King Charles I gave a grant of 1200 merks to the Reverend Ewan Cameron, minister of Dunoon, 200 of which were to be given annually to a schoolmaster. Fifty-four years later, in 1695, reference was made in the records of the Parish Church in Dunoon of a salary paid to a dominie. That old word for a school master conveys a great deal to those educated in Scotland. The dominie was much more than just a schoolteacher, for he was very much a personal mentor to his pupils, caring for every aspect of their lives. He was usually a much respected and loved figure in the locality where he taught.

It was the custom in those days for the schoolmaster to teach pupils in his own home, which was usually a small thatched cottage. Similar places of learning were to be found at Kilmun, Toward and Dalinlongart at the head of Holy Loch. School would begin at five or six in the morning during the summer, and at sunrise in the winter, going on until six in the evening with a short break at noon.

At Dunoon, the schoolmaster was usually Session Clerk, Precentor and Registrar of baptisms and marriages, and was therefore able to supplement his annual income of about £11 by charging twopence for each of these services.

Recalcitrant boys were fairly harshly disciplined in those days. Two boys who had broken into a garden at Kilmun were not considered old enough to be 'told off' before the congregation at church, which was the usual form of adult punishment, so instead they were put in the 'jougs'. These were iron collars with chains, which were fastened to the churchyard wall, and were not just limited to use for the young, as in 1696 two women had this severe sentence meted out to them.

In 1768 so many pupils were attending lessons in Dunoon that the dominie's cottage became too small to accommodate them. The school, therefore, transferred to the church. This, however, did not last long as the boys vandalised part of the building, as well as tearing up a good number of the pews. It was decided to move the children to the upper part of a house adjoining the church (now part of the Glasgow Hotel) and it was there that John McPharlane taught for about sixteen years.

It was usual for the teacher to give his scholars a 'wee dram' every Candlemas, and this continued until about 1770. Another tradition was the unattractive one of cock fighting. Excited schoolboys could be seen walking to their classes carrying a cock, its spurs already sharpened for the combat. The teacher was happy to take part in this cruel sport as he was allowed to keep the birds after the fight.

At that time, the schoolmaster was responsible for keeping the church clock in working order and ensuring its speedy repair if it went wrong. This would bring him an extra five shillings a year.

In more remote areas winter schools existed at the end of the eighteenth century. This involved children, from between twelve and fifteen years of age, going from house to house teaching younger children. They would receive about twenty shillings a year, as well as their food and lodging.

In school the children were responsible for supplying their own paper and writing materials. In some instances they even arrived at school with peat to help heat the classroom. Colonel Campbell of Ballochyle reminisced about this aspect of school life in his talk to the Glasgow Cowal Society in 1872. "My eldest brother Alexander used to go to the old schoolhouse at Kilmun with my cousin, both with their peats under their arms as contributions to the school fire! I wonder what folk would say nowadays to the Laird's eldest son going to school with a peat under his arm."

In those days conditions were spartan. Open fires provided the heat, and lighting was by gas. Desks were twelve feet long and the children sat on backless chairs.

By 1811 there were sufficient pupils to warrant a school – and master's house – in Dunoon. So in 1876 the Primary School, fronting on to Tom-a-Mhoid Road, was built, a second storey being added in 1894. In 1907 what was called 'the new school' – the Secondary School for twelve- to eighteen-year-old children was added, its frontage on Hillfoot Street.

It is to the school's credit that it was one of the first in Scotland to employ a woman teacher, and in 1897 one of the earliest women graduates, Charlotte Tweedie MA, was engaged to teach French and German.

To many people the Grammar School of the 1890s and early 1900s is synonymous with William Dock, its much respected and loved headmaster. Dock was a most exceptional man and had a place in the heart of many ex-pupils. He came to Dunoon from Paisley in about 1895 and immediately made his mark on the community.

Dunoon Grammar School

Army Cadet Corps training at Dunoon Grammar School in Hillfoot Street in 1912. Rector William Dock is the master on the extreme right of the picture

Robert Shiach remembered the dominie as "A tall upright figure, well over six feet in his academic gown and mortar-board hat. Since he always had rubber heels on his shoes he seemed to swish along the corridors as silently as a breath of wind!"

Robert Shiach went on to recall, "We always called him 'Billy' among ourselves. He was a good disciplinarian but always very fair, and he had the complete trust and love of us all. He was a bachelor and lived in the schoolhouse, which was situated in the school grounds at the west end of Castle Street, under the care of a housekeeper."

Robert's schooldays were partly during the First World War when it was quite usual for members of the Armed Forces, who had been Dock's former pupils, to call at the school during their leaves to see their old headmaster. William was so pleased to have these old boys visiting him that he would take them round several classes in the senior school to 'show them off'. Some of the men would look very self-conscious when Dock told the classroom of their misdemeanours or scholastic abilities during their schooldays. Many of these servicemen would come to Dunoon just for a day, and it was Dock's invariable practice to go down to the pier to see them off. He did not even take off his academic gown or his mortar-board. Amazed visitors would see this tall, dignified schoolmaster accompany a lad in uniform down to the waiting steamer.

When William Dock retired at the age of sixty-five in 1925, a number of his old boys, of whom Robert Shiach was one, gave a special luncheon for him in Glasgow, a gesture which was repeated in 1945 on his eighty-fifth birthday. Although retired, Dock would return to the school as Rector Emeritus on most Prize-Giving days and continued to do so until well into his nineties.

When he left the school, the Rector bought a house in Edinburgh which he named The Gantocks after the rocks near his home in Dunoon. Like many of his ex-pupils, Robert Shiach, who was working in Edinburgh, used to visit him as often as possible and always received the greatest courtesy and kindness, not only from the dominie, but also from his housekeeper, Miss Drummond. Dock had engaged Miss Drummond when he came to Edinburgh in 1925, giving her the appropriate wage for the time.

Robert remembered visiting him one evening in 1950 and during the course of conversation William said, "Do you know, Robert, I'm having a lot of trouble with Miss Drummond these days." He leaned over very confidentially and continued, "Miss Drummond does not think that £1 per week is enough wage for a housekeeper." The poor woman had not had an increase for twenty-five years! However Miss Drummond stayed with William until his death and fell heir to his house and furniture.

In the late 1950s the school had a serious fire, and it was decided that the Primary and Secondary schools should be separated. So on Friday 13th March 1964 the Secondary Department of the new Grammar School at Ardenslate Road was formally opened by the Secretary of State for Scotland, Michael Noble MP.

The Grammar School has produced men and women of many talents, a great number of whom have become famous throughout the world. It is noteworthy that in 1983 three out of the seventy-one Scottish MPs in the House of Commons were educated at Dunoon Grammar School: The Rt. Hon. John Smith, son of a former headmaster of the Primary School, George Robertson and John Mackay, now Lord Mackay of Ardbrecknish. At the time of writing another ex-pupil, Brian Wilson is a Member of Parliament.

Also included in the political roll-call is a former Prime Minister of Queensland, Australia – W Forgan-Smith.

In Melbourne, Australia, a former pupil, Bishop James Grant, while attending a Book Fair in 1981, discovered a little booklet entitled *The Dunoon Story* . He bought it thinking it was about his former home where his late father had been engineer at the waterworks. He was intensely surprised to find it was all about a village in the north of New South Wales, which was founded in the late 1870s by Duncan Currie, who gave the name of his birthplace to the scrubland he had claimed. Duncan cleared the 640 acres and developed it and today it is a small settlement of three hundred persons with a general store, post office and garage.

One well-known Scottish clergyman who is among the Grammar School's ex-pupils is the Rev Dr Donald C Caskie, who became known as the 'Tartan Pimpernel' during the Second World War and wrote about his experiences in a book of the same title.

During the war Donald was minister of the Scots Kirk in Paris, and when the Germans entered the city he escaped to the South of France. There, he ran an underground 'get you home' scheme for British and Allied Servicemen caught in France after the fall of Dunkirk.

Caskie was responsible for the repatriation of many soldiers, sailors and airmen through Spain, and was imprisoned and sentenced to death by the Gestapo. Luckily, the death sentence was lifted in 1944. He served with the famous hero, Lieutenant Commander Pat O'Leary RN, one of the war's most brilliant underground leaders who was awarded the George Cross for his valiant services.

A more recent hero was ex-pupil Captain Hector Connell who was given the MBE in 1981. Hector rescued Vietnamese refugees from the South China Sea while in command of the bulk carrier *Wellpark*. There were three hundred and fifty Vietnamese in an overloaded launch, and despite poor weather the Captain managed to get them all aboard his ship where they were looked after until their safe arrival in Taiwan.

Paul Hutton went to the Grammar School in the days when A. E. Smith was Rector and also scoutmaster of the Dunoon Scout Troop. Paul recalled that Mr Smith organised some of the best Gang Shows at the Cosy Corner that Dunoon had ever seen or was likely to see again.

In 1991 Dunoon Grammar School celebrated its 350th anniversary with a splendid dinner which was attended by many ex-pupils, some of whom had come from far distant places. The Guest of Honour was John Smith MP, later to become leader of the Labour Party. A month after John Smith's untimely death in 1994, George Robertson MP, another former pupil and then Shadow Secretary of State for Scotland, gave a speech at the annual prizegiving. He movingly paid tribute to his friend and colleague, one of Dunoon Grammar School's most illustrious pupils.

Today, the Grammar School's Rector is Joseph Rhodes MA who, when he was appointed, was the youngest man ever to hold such a post in Scotland.

21

They do but Visit and Away

ONE OF DUNOON'S earliest and most important visitors was Mary Queen of Scots. In 1563 the Queen decided to tour the west of Scotland which, so far, was unknown to her. It was in July of that year that she went to stay with her half-sister, the Duchess of Argyll at Inverary Castle. The Duke, as laid down in a Royal Charter granted by King James III to his ancestor Colin Campbell of Argyll in 1472, was Hereditary Keeper of Dunoon Castle. This entitled him to the attached feudal rights and the gift of some of the neighbouring lands. As rent for the castle the keeper was required to present a red rose to the reigning monarch as a token of rent whenever he or she arrived in Dunoon.

En route to the Campbell stronghold at Dunoon, Queen Mary with her entourage, accompanied by the Duke and Duchess of Argyll, stayed at Strachur and the following day, Tuesday 27th July, arrived at Dunoon Castle where she spent the night. The next day, all of which was spent at Dunoon, the Queen was presented with the traditional red rose by the Master of the Household. On the 29th, the anniversary of the date in 1565 that Mary had married Lord Darnley at Holyrood Palace, the Queen had dinner at Dunoon, and then moved on to Toward Castle for an overnight stay. She was received by Sir James Lamont who had ready for her the best quarters, which were in the recently erected Hall-house. Sir James had felt that the kitchen would not be adequate to cater for the whole Court, so had installed an enormous fireplace and chimney to improve the cooking facilities.

While staying at Toward, Queen Mary planted a tree which survived until the time that Kirkman Finlay acquired the land. No one seems to know whether it was cut down or fell during a severe gale.

The Queen dined with Sir James on the Friday, and afterwards one of his galleys transported her and the retinue across the Firth to the Ayrshire coast for the continuation of the Royal Tour.

The next royal occasion on the Clyde was when Queen Victoria, in August 1847, was on board the Royal Yacht *Victoria and Albert*

The West of Scotland Convalescent Home, Dunoon was kept by subscription from Clyde shipyards and factory workers. In World War II the Royal Navy took over the homes and renamed them HMS *Osprey*

moored off Greenock. The yacht had been escorted to the Tail of the Bank by a fleet of river steamers and a multitude of small craft. It was a memorable occasion with enthusiastic crowds along the shoreline cheering as she sailed by.

The first royal visit to Dunoon since that of Mary, Queen of Scots, was on 5th August 1872 when Queen Victoria's daughter HRH the Princess Louise and her husband, the Marquis of Lorne, visited the West of Scotland Convalescent Seaside Homes just outside the town's main street on the Sandbank Road.

But undoubtedly the greatest royal honour to be bestowed on Dunoon was the visit of Queen Elizabeth II and the Duke of Edinburgh in 1958 when they were visiting the Clyde in the Royal Yacht *Britannia*. On 11th August the royal couple stepped ashore at Dunoon pier where they were greeted by local dignitaries. Huge crowds thronged the promenade and Castle Gardens to greet them.

Elizabeth Burgess remembered that visit extremely well. "It was a great day for Dunoon. The Queen was officially to open the new Pavilion. Two rows of chairs were placed outside the Hall for the elderly, so my mother and my friend's father sat in style waiting for Her Majesty to arrive. There were many visitors and residents, all eager to witness the opening.

"The Argyll and Sutherland Highlanders, who had received the Freedom of the Burgh of Dunoon five years previously, stood silently outside the Hall waiting for the Queen to inspect the regiment. All of a sudden a little dog appeared from the crowd, walked across the parade ground, cocked a leg and did the necessary against a soldier's trousers. There was great laughter in the crowd, but I do not think the soldier was amused. He never moved a muscle, but he must have been very embarrassed. The little dog disappeared into the crowd, amid great laughter, just as the Queen arrived."

The Queen then unveiled a commemorative panel at the new Pavilion which thereafter was called Queen's Hall.

After the ceremony and the signing of the Visitor's Book, the Queen went to the Castle Gardens where she was met at the entrance by the Captain of Dunstaffnage, Michael E. Campbell, wearing a kilt of the Campbell tartan and a brick-red jacket. Bare-headed and holding his royal blue bonnet topped with a dark red rose, he duly offered it to Her Majesty in token of rent. The Captain of Dunstaffnage explained that he was presenting the rose on behalf of the Duke of Argyll, Hereditary Keeper of Dunoon Castle.

Another honour for the town was the visit of HRH the Duchess of Gloucester for the official opening of Dunoon and District General Hospital in November 1966. The Duchess, accompanied by her lady-in-waiting, Miss Jean Maxwell-Scott, arrived at the sports stadium in a helicopter of the Queen's Flight. At the hospital there were crowds waiting to see Her Royal Highness unveil the Commemorative Window, designed by Avril Gibb from Skelmorlie.

A more recent royal visitor was HRH The Princess Royal who came to Dunoon in October 1989. As President of the Riding for the Disabled Association, Princess Anne, after a buffet lunch at the Enmore Hotel, visited the Woodside Group of the Association in Innellan. There she watched the riders and talked to staff.

Over the years many writers, poets, musicians and artists have visited Dunoon. Elizabeth Gaskell, who wrote that marvellously sensitive study of village life, *Cranford*, was working extremely hard on the biography of her friend Charlotte Brontë, and the only break she allowed herself was a visit in the autumn of 1855 to various relatives in Scotland. One of these was a duty visit to her half-sister Catherine who lived in Dunoon.

The Edinburgh-born poet, novelist and essayist, Robert Louis Stevenson came several times to Dunoon. As a youngster he stayed at a house called Rosmore (now Park Lea) in Auchamore Road adjoining the site of the farm where 'Highland Mary' was born.

His second visit was in 1870 when he was still studying to be an engineer, a career which he abandoned for the Law, becoming an advocate in 1875. Stevenson never practised but took up his pen to become author of such well-known and loved novels as *Kidnapped, Treasure Island* and the *Master of Ballantrae*. His slim volume of poems, *A Child's Garden of Verses*, is a great favourite with the young.

His father, Thomas Stevenson, was engineer to the Board of Northern Lighthouses and in all likelihood Robert Louis was sent to Dunoon to represent his father's firm on the contract connected with the town's new pier.

In March 1881 the first number of *Quiz*, the humorous periodical, was published in Glasgow. It lasted for twenty years, and the design on the cover was by Martin Anderson, afterwards to become widely known as Cynicus, a frequent contributor to the paper. Later he became prominent as a satiric artist and publisher of postcards.

One summer in the 1870s Cynicus and a friend, Joseph Tatlow, spent a month at Dunoon. They attended a fancy-dress ball where Cynicus made sketches of the most important people present and, of course, the prettiest girls. Early next morning he took the first steamer across the Firth and had six hundred copies of his drawings run off in Glasgow. That evening he was back at Dunoon selling the lithographs at threepence each, making a profit of £4!

A frequent visitor to the Cowal shore in the late 1800s and early 1900s was the novelist, poet and journalist, Neil Munro. Born in Inveraray in 1864, Munro knew the West Highland folk better than any other writer, and drew upon them in those whimsical and amusing tales *Para Handy*.

Travelling people and tinkers were always very much part of the scene in Dunoon. Isabella MacVicar remembered when she was a little girl a man with an organ and a monkey coming to town every year. "He was an Italian with a long, big moustache, and I was absolutely terrified of him. He always used to come into the big courtyard near the stables at Torr-Aluinn, and I used to go and kick him and then run away. Then there was the dancing bear. The man with him had a big hat on his head with bells tinkling round, and a drum on his back. He was a one-man band and every time he lifted his foot a string attached to it would produce a thump on the drum. One year, Old Chess, the policeman from Strachur, accompanied him with his accordian. Duncan, a friend of ours, was looking out of the window to see the bear, and he shouted to his wife, 'Would you come and see the bear dancing?' And she ran to watch. 'Oh,' she said, 'just like a human being.' 'Get away with you woman,' Duncan said, 'He's no more like a human being than I am!'

"Then there was the Bunt family who came every year from Wales. They had a beautiful caravan with lovely brasswork, always bright and polished. They travelled the whole of the country, but spent a lot of time in the Dunoon area. They would go to the Gas Work lane at Innellan and park and camp on the beach. I used to love to see them and get to look in at the caravan with the lace curtains. They made marvellous baskets, and whatever you wanted, they would have it. We got to know these people very well and they were quiet folk. Then, of course, we had the tinks, plenty of them. Quite different from the travelling people."

David Beveridge had memories of the tinkers. He recalled, "Old Collins, of Clear Type Press, used to buy bricks from the tinks, the McPhees, who used to steal the same bricks from him and resell them!"

Jane MacLaren remembered the McPhees' greatest rivals, the Johnstons, who used to play their bagpipes to the holiday visitors and rounded the purse on Saturday nights getting as "fu as a wilk".

Donald Macdonald recalled walking along the East Bay one day in the 1930s and seeing a debauched looking and 'well-lubricated' man coming towards him. It turned out to be Jim Mollison, the aviator and husband of that great flying woman Amy Johnson. Amy had flown, in 1930, alone from Croydon, England, to Australia in nineteen-and-a-half days, but her greatest aeronautical achievement was her flight in 1936 to the Cape, South Africa, and back, beating by ten-and-a-half hours the record set by Mollison in 1932.

David Brechin, a Dunoon man living in South Africa, was out one day shooting near the Modder river by Magersfontein, which was well-known for the battles in which the Argyll and Sutherland Highlanders, with heavy losses, took part during the Boer War. After the war many Scottish families emigrated to South Africa. David wrote, "I was crossing a big field bordering a farm near the river, when I passed a clump of trees heavily enclosed by barbed wire and a padlocked gate. It was an old graveyard. From the other side of the fence I was just able to make out some of the inscriptions. They were of people born in Dunoon who had farmed there many years before. It was a moving moment to stand there in the silence of the veld broken only by the scream of a fish eagle from a blue gum near the river, and see the graves of people with grand old Highland names buried so many miles from their homeland."

Mrs R. Logan, when young in the 1920s and early 1930s, used to holiday with her family in Dunoon. She remembered with nostalgia coming off the Craigendoran steamer at Dunoon pier and getting into a landau (an open horse-drawn carriage) which took her and the family to Mrs McNair in Auchamore Road. John McNair had a boating station in West Bay where he hired out rowing boats and the young folk used to spend most of their time helping him haul up or launch the boats. John used to row over to the Gantock rocks for mussels, as he swore they were the best fish bait.

May Gallacher, too, had fond memories of Dunoon in the 1930s. "At the height of the season, I can tell you the place was something then. Ice-cream barrows, candy stalls, and mussel and whelks barrows all along the front. Then there was the bike store where you could hire all sorts of bicycles, two-wheelers or three-wheelers, for one shilling an hour. Ice-cream cones were the size of tennis balls, all for just fourpence."

Jenny Mathieson, a native of Dunoon, also remembered the time when the town was a 'swinging place'. Jenny and her friends used to meet for coffee and a 'blather' at Juno's café on the front. It was run by the Giarchis, an Italian family, and was one of the most popular meeting places in the town.

Janet Vint used to come regularly to Dunoon for her summer holidays until the mid-1950s. She boarded with a Mrs Helen Chisholm in Argyll Road. "Mrs Chisholm had great psychic powers. She used her gift to read one's hand, cup or sand, and was a really first-class profess-ional. When I was sixteen she told me that I would have three children. In my twenties I had two girls and when I was almost forty-three I had a son.

"Mrs Chisholm became a familiar sight at Cowal Highland Gather-ings where she had a tent in which she used her clairvoyance on people wishing to know their future. She never took a penny from anyone, giving all the money she earned to local charities."

A well-known visitor, remembered by Deborah Mitchell, was Mr Knowles who came from Clydebank. For almost twenty years during the summer months before the Second World War, Mr Knowles would come to Dunoon at the beginning of June when he used to board with Deborah's grandmother, Mrs Somerville, of George Street. He was a tall, striking figure with white hair and a waxed moustache and looked very impressive when, wearing full Highland regalia and his black brogues with silver buckles (which Deborah polished for sixpence a week) he would march along the promenade, playing his bagpipes. Then the war came, and after the night of the Clydebank Blitz, Mrs Somerville and Deborah never heard from him again and assumed that he had been killed during the ferocious bombardment.

Over the years politicians of every persuasion have come to visit Dunoon and the surrounding villages and hamlets to campaign for their particular parties; sometimes they have come on fact-finding missions or to attend some noteworthy function; and, of course, sometimes they simply came for a holiday.

A person of particular interest to visit the town in the summer of 1975 was the grandson of the first Provost of Dunoon, Archibald Mitchell. Also called Archibald he met the town's last Provost, John Thomson, who was in office from 1974-1975. John Thomson presented Archibald Mitchell with a book on Dunoon's Centenary as a Burgh, inscribing it 'From the last Provost to the first Provost's Grandson'. A poignant occasion.

Elizabeth Rankin expressed with great affection what so many visitors and expatriates feel about Dunoon and its lovely surrounding country-side.

"In my late teens my father's cousin bought a house in Argyll Road. It was a little bit out of the town and very nice, so she used to ask my sister and me, and one or other of my aunts who lived with us, to come and stay for holidays. In this way we got to know Dunoon very well. This cousin, although in her late seventies, was a great walker and she took us all around the district, even to Sandbank and Puck's Glen, and over in the ferry to Kilmun.

"We visited the old churches and cemeteries and she used to amuse us by saying she didn't want to be buried in Dunoon for on the 'Last Day' they would all get up and talk Gaelic and she wouldn't know what they were saying!

"I grew to love Dunoon and especially the walk up past the water-works to see the wonderful view over the town and the Clyde, with the Gantocks and the Cloch in the distance. I sometimes tried to paint that view, but my efforts weren't very good.

"Morag's Fairy Glen was another of my favourite haunts. I loved its rustic beauty. I think we paid sixpence to enter it, but I'm not sure.

"As we grew older we often met some of our friends who also came here and we all walked along the promenade which was packed with people in July and August. Of course, we also met boys who were there on holiday, and we all went for walks or danced at night in the Castle Gardens which were like fairyland with lights strung all over and in the trees. There were also mysterious little paths leading off the main one where we danced, and some little nooks where you could sit, or kiss and cuddle if you wanted to.

"The Gardens were very popular in daytime, too, with all ages of people. You could sit up there and look over the pier which was a very bustling place. All day long steamers were coming and going. What we particularly loved were the evening excursions with dancing on board, and the steamers that organised mystery trips.

"Along the promenade there were many kiosks selling ices, but our favourite one was near the pier where we sat and consumed such delights as Knickerbocker Glory or Mary in the Garden.

"There used to be dozens of boat-hirers along the beach on the West Bay, as many as twenty in the 1950s, and you could take a boat out for an hour or so at very little cost.

"If you didn't want to bathe in the sea you could go to the Lido, but there were many little coves among the trees and bushes which grew out along the Innellan Road and were ideal for sunbathing.

"In those days the whole town had a great air of gaiety about it, especially on the Saturday in August when the Cowal Games were held.

The march along Argyll Street of a thousand pipers was something marvellous to see. I remember seeing Sir Harry Lauder with his niece at the Games, presenting some of the cups to the fortunate winners. The World Pipe Band Contest was held there, and at the end of the Games all the bands came down a slope on to the field playing their pipes and drums. What a wonderful sight and sound.

"I think my happiest time was just a month before the Second World War started. Four of us were going on holiday; my girlfriend and I and the boy I later married, and his friend. This was quite a daring thing to do in those days, but my girlfriend and I had a room in Dunoon, while the boys were camping outside town.

"The highlight of this wonderful holiday was the fantastic fireworks display which always marked the close of the Cowal Games. We sat up on the little hill behind Highland Mary's statue among tightly packed bodies. There were thousands of people watching all around the pier. It was as though we all knew that we'd never see Dunoon again as it was then.

"During the war I visited Dunoon with my husband on one of our leaves from the army. There was a boom across the Clyde from the Cloch to the Gantocks, and we watched the destroyers on the river and sadly thought of the dear old paddle steamers with their colourful bunting and their bands playing cheery music.

"Our last visit was just after my husband was demobbed from the army in 1946. We came for a week's holiday with our fourteen-month-old baby and stayed at the Glasgow Hotel overlooking the pier. It was in March, and the sea was wild. We were the only visitors in the hotel and the chef (who had been in the navy) and his wife, were looking after the hotel during the off-season, and made us feel very welcome and were very good to us.

"It was a very nostalgic holiday, but it could never be the same again."

22

"All the People Like Us are We"

THE ABOVE QUOTATION from Rudyard Kipling's poem continues, "And Everyone Else is They". This is really how all natives and residents of a town or village feel towards 'incomers', and this chapter is about people who lived in Dunoon or spent so much of the year in the town that they considered themselves to be part of it.

The MacArthur-Moirs were very well-known in Dunoon, and today can be seen streets named after members of the family – MacArthur, Moir, John, Jane, Mary, and Alexander, to name just a few. There was a John MacArthur living at Arthurhall as early as 1652. Arthurhall was a few yards north of the present Milton House, and John MacArthur-Moir started feuing the land on the Milton Estate in about 1822.

At one time most of the big villas along the coast were owned by wealthy Glaswegians who used them during the summer. The owners were men who had made their fortunes in shipping, engineering, construction, tea, tobacco, sugar and cotton. Among them were the well-known manufacturers, kings of their particular trades, like J. Templeton whose carpet factory, opposite the People's Palace in Glasgow Green, is a replica of the Doges Palace in Venice; and the large Coats family, the thread makers of Paisley.

William Coats lived at Willow Bank in Auchamore Road and the family were founders and supporters of Dunoon's Baptist Church, keeping eight seats in it, as well as eight seats in Holy Trinity Church.

But there were other people of equal interest – those in the arts and professions, and ordinary folk who often were much more colourful and entertaining than their better-known neighbours.

An interesting man who lived in the town was Rowland East, a surgeon, who believed in hydropathic medicine. This is a treatment to cure diseases by water, used outward and inwardly, and dates back to about 1829 when an Austrian farmer from Silesia, Vincenz Priessmitz, began his public career by extending his farm so as to accommodate the increasing number of people attracted by the fame of the treatment.

Water, however, played an important part in the life of Dunoon. In 1975 Mary Waite and her husband Robert discovered an old well in the garden of their house in George Street. The sixty-foot well contained the most remarkably pure water that they had ever tasted, and people thought that it contained 'miraculous qualities', curing migraines, arthritis and rheumatic pains. The well's reputation spread far and wide, even across the ocean to the United States, and visitors called on the Waites all the year round to drink the water or fill containers to take back home with them.

In 1864 Professor Robert Buchanan came to Dunoon to retire and live in Ardfillayne. Born in Callander in 1785 Buchanan studied Divinity at Glasgow University, and then in 1827 became the University's Professor of Logic, thereby earning the nickname of 'Logic Bob'. He was the author of many books, poems and plays. Robert bequeathed in his will £10,000 for the founding of bursaries in connection with the University Arts Classes. He died in March 1873 and was buried in Dunoon.

Poets were much attracted to Dunoon and the Cowal Peninsula. One of these was William Cameron, born on 3rd December 1801 in Dunipace Parish, Stirlingshire, where his father was in the woollen trade.

In the late 1830s William came to Dunoon where he lived in Gowan Lea, a cottage in Wellington Street. It was here that he wrote many songs and poems, some about Dunoon, including *The Balgy Burn* and, of course, his most famous poem about the area, *Morag's Faery Glen*.

Torr-Aluinn was built by an English wine importer whose son, Sir Francis Powell (1833-1914) became famous as a watercolour artist, and is best known for his landscapes and marine paintings. In 1878 Francis Powell (who was to be knighted in 1893) became one of the founders, and the first President, of the Royal Scottish Water-Colour Society in Glasgow, the opening of which was attended by Queen Victoria.

Isabella MacVicar whose father, Mr Black, was gardener at Torr-Aluinn, had many memories of the artist whom she found a charming, very quiet, gentle and reticent man. Isabella recalled, "In the house there were only Sir Francis and his wife and three of an indoor staff. There was also a coachman for two horses, my father and a general handyman. Eventually the horses were done away with and they had a motor car, an Argyll, similar to the one owned by the Finlays of Castle Toward."

After the death of his wife Sir Francis courted his young model, Annie MacNab. Annie's father was a gardener at the house of Alice Gasgoigne, Sir Francis's aunt. Isabella used to accompany the artist when he went to fetch Annie every morning. "Sir Francis used to take me with him – I was a little girl then – and hold my hand. Then we

(above) Francis Powell, the famous Victorian watercolour artist, lived at Torr-Aluinn, Innellan

(below) Jessie McLachlan, widely considered to be falsely convicted in the Sandyford murder case

returned with Annie, and she would get ready for the painting session in the studio at the top of the house. While she was preparing herself Sir Francis would take me into his study, sit me on his knee and open his desk, where he always kept a tin of Clarnico caramels. I knew I only had to put my finger in one of the little pigeon holes and pull out a small envelope to find in it four caramels, one for each of my parents, my sister and myself. I used to lick the envelope down and borrow Sir Francis' rubber stamp and stamp on the envelope 'Torr-Aluinn, Dunoon, Argyll'."

When Sir Francis and Annie married he was eighty-one and she was twenty-three!

Isabella's husband, Donald MacVicar, had a story to tell about Schor-behan, the house owned by the Lockitt's, Sir Francis's first wife's parents. It was later bought by Jimmy Reid. Nicknamed 'Scotch Jimmy', Jimmy was a professional burglar and in the summer he used to throw huge parties to which he invited people from all the neighbouring districts. When the house was crammed with guests he would sneak out of the house and burgle his guests' homes. Unfortunately Donald was unable to relate how 'Scotch Jimmy' finally was found out.

There was another Dunoon resident as undesirable as 'Scotch Jimmy,' and that was James Fleming who lived in a house between Dunoon and Innellan called Avondale Lodge. Fleming was involved in one of the most sensational murder trials of the nineteenth century, which aroused deep passions throughout the entire country.

James Fleming, his son James, and his grandson, lived in Sandyford Place near Charing Cross, a district of Glasgow favoured at the time by the medical profession. The two younger members of the Fleming family used the house as a *pied à terre* during the week and usually spent weekends at Avondale Lodge.

On Friday 4th July 1862, James Fleming and his son went to their office in St Vincent Street, leaving eighty-seven-year-old Grandpa Fleming alone with the maid Jessie McPherson. Jessie had often told her friends her life was miserable, and she described old James Fleming as 'an old wretch and an old deevil'.

That Friday the two younger Flemings decided to

go to Dunoon directly from the office and did not return to Glasgow until the following Monday, when they went straight to St Vincent Street. Late on Monday afternoon the grandson returned to the house in Sandyford Place and was surprised when his grandfather opened the door instead of Jessie. He asked where the maid was and Mr Fleming said he had not seen her since Friday, and when he had tried to find her discovered her bedroom door was locked. The young Fleming immediately asked if his grandfather had not considered the possibility of Jessie being dead, to which the older man replied, 'Dead or not dead, she's away.' Then James Fleming arrived, and on being told what had happened decided to break down Jessie's bedroom door to see if she was all right. She definitely was not! She was lying, face downwards on the floor, beside her bed. Except for the upper part of her body, which was covered with a dark cloth, the girl was almost naked. Jessie McPherson was dead.

The doctor was called, and on examining the woman found forty wounds all over her body, as well as a remarkable bruise on the lower part of her back. The police were then summoned and declared that Jessie had been murdered.

Grandpa Fleming made a statement, which at the time was not believed by the police, and he was arrested. Somehow, he managed to involve Mrs Jessie McLachlan, a friend of Jessie's. Mrs McLachlan's cause was not helped by the fact that she had pawned some of the Fleming silver and had in her possession one of the dead woman's dresses. Fleming was released and became the Crown's Chief Witness. Jessie McLachlan was arrested and, after a lengthy trial, sentenced to death.

On leaving the Court after giving his evidence, Fleming was greeted by a hostile and jeering crowd. He left for the relative peace of Avondale Lodge in Dunoon, but popular indignation followed him there, and this 'usually quiet and decorative place' became the scene of more hostile demonstrations. During the time Jessie was in jail, old Fleming used to lurk behind the bushes at Avondale Lodge and mutter to passing commuters, "Have they no' hangit that wumman yet?"

The circumstances of the case were such that public opinion felt that the death penalty should not be carried out. In almost every town throughout the country meetings of protest were held and petitions signed for Jessie's death sentence to be commuted. At the time opinion was that James Fleming was the guilty man, which undoubtedly he was, for there had been a drunken evening in the basement at Sandyford Place with Jessie McPherson and her friend Jessie McLachlan and old Fleming. Jessie McLachlan had been sent out for more alcohol, during which the first assault must have taken place, and the murder most likely completed during another of her brief absences from the house. The case was discussed in the House of Commons and, owing to immense public pressure, the Home Secretary commuted the death sentence to that of life imprisonment.

In October 1877 Jessie McLachlan, aged forty-four, was released from Perth General Prison where she had been an exemplary inmate. Two years later, she and her son emigrated to America, where she remarried and lived a private and peaceful life to the end of her days.

James Tod was an interesting Dunoon resident. He was an engineer and well-known in the mid-1800s to a generation of Atlantic travellers with the Daman Line.

He was engineer to the *City of Baltimor e* which had been bought by the French Government to carry troops between Marseilles and the Crimea during the war. Tod was horrified at the suffering of the soldiers during the first terrible winter of the Crimean conflict in 1854, and had many stories to relate about that ghastly episode.

James was in the engine room of the *City of Brussels* when she was run down by the *Kirby Hall* on 7th January 1885. On that occasion 'Jimmie', as he was known to American travellers, behaved with great coolness, and while floating among wreckage in the ice-cold water, told comic stories to his fellow sufferers in order to keep their morale up until they were rescued. James Tod died in his house, Harthill, in 1904 after a full and eventful life.

Isabella Villa was the home of W. W. Mackay who became Dunoon's Provost in 1891. He was most generous to the town, presenting it with a new gas lamp at Ferry Brae, two fountains, and a semi-grand piano to be used in the Burgh Hall. This gift, however, had a string attached to it. Mackay laid down the condition that "the piano will not be let, say, for Negro comic songs or dances or any kind of buffoonery; but I would leave it to those who let the Hall to decide, knowing my mind, what they think would be of a lowering moral tendence, and ask them to refuse the use of it only to such. I think it should not be let for dancing purposes after eleven o'clock at night, except on very rare occasions."

In 1900 the Provost surely gave the town one of its most useful gifts — £500 for the purpose of having teeth extracted free.

In 1887 was born William Forgan-Smith, who came to live in Dunoon when his father became head-gardener at Muirend Estate in Bullwood. Forgan-Smith went to Dunoon Grammar School and then on to school in Glasgow, but his formal education came abruptly to a halt when he refused family pressure to go into the Church. Instead he became apprenticed as a painter and decorator in Glasgow, although at one stage he spent time as a labourer in the Clydeside shipyards. It was during his days in Glasgow that William made frequent visits to Glasgow Green to hear Keir Hardie and other politicians, and it was from them that his interest in politics grew.

He left Scotland in 1911, and by the following year was well settled in Mackay, a sugar-producing town, in North Queensland, Australia. Soon Forgan-Smith became involved in local politics and before long was Vice-President of the Mackay Trades and Labour Council. In 1915 the first election in Queensland with compulsory voting took place, and Forgan-Smith contested the safe Nationalist Party seat of Mackay, and very soon began a rapid rise through the Parliamentary ranks, initially being the Labour Party's chief spokesman on the sugar industry.

John Mackay, living in North Mackay, recalled an early election. "Bill Smith, as he was known in those days, decided to stand as the Labour member for Mackay, but had to unseat the Liberal or Tory member, a Dr Knott. The doctor remarked when he saw Bill painting the Harbour Board Flagpole that it was a foretaste of his chances in the Election – 'He would be up the pole!' Bill congratulated him and said if the learned doctor had looked a little closer he would have seen the Knotts being painted out! Not only did Bill win that election, but on 17th June 1932 he became Premier of Queensland, a position he held until 1942. Apart from the present incumbent he was Queensland's longest serving Premier. On his retirement from active politics Bill took up various posts in the sugar industry and became Chancellor of the State University." William Forgan-Smith died on 25th September 1953 greatly mourned by his many friends in Dunoon.

Francis George Scott, the composer, was born in 1880 in Hawick. It was the anniversary of the birth of Robert Burns, 25th January, and years later Scott was to set many of the poet's lyrics to music.

In 1912 Scott came to Dunoon on the advice of his doctor who thought the sea air would be beneficial. For two years he taught in the Grammar School. One of his previous pupils had been Christopher Murray Grieve, the son of a postman. Grieve, as Hugh MacDiarmid, contributed much to Scottish poetry, and was a founder member of the Scottish National Party.

Primarily a composer of songs, Francis George Scott also wrote the orchestral suite *The Seven Deadly Sins*, and *Lament for Heroes* among other works.

Stuart Peck had many memories of life as a boy in and around Dunoon in the 1920s and 1930s. His maternal grandparents, Dr William and Mrs Hay, owned a house in Bullwood. Dr Hay, born some time in the 1840s, had taken Holy Orders and became the first Minister of the Kirk in Johannesburg, South Africa. On his return home he became a physician, and retired to Avondale (previously Avondale Lodge, home of the Fleming family) where Stuart remembered, "One room of the house was fitted up as a surgery with all sorts of medicines and stomach pumps and that sort of thing."

But it was the garden that Stuart loved. "The garden was notable for a unique two-storied, octagonal summerhouse designed to look like a Chinese pagoda. In the upper storey was an old bicycle-wheel which I used to 'steer', imagining myself to be on my own ship's bridge, having one mighty sea adventure after another. We called the summerhouse naturally, The Pagoda, and I remember grandfather's old Highland gardener calling it The Padoga in his soft Highland accent. 'Chust that,' he would say when I was asking if he had something I had mislaid, 'I think you would be finding it in the Padoga.' When I was recuperating from a serious illness, a bed was made up for me on the upper floor of this fascinating summerhouse, and I was able to watch all the shipping pass up and down the Clyde, including the famous liner *Empress of Britain* which at the time was doing her sea trails."

One of Stuart Peck's grandmother's brothers, Sir John Ure Primrose, a Glasgow grain merchant, was Lord Provost of the City in 1902, following in the footsteps of his uncle, John Ure, who had been Provost in 1880. Sir John's son, Sir William Primrose, lived in a neighbouring house Garail (now a home for the elderly) with the little burn, the Gar, running through the garden. It was the only house in Bullwood, when Stuart was a child, that had any form of electricity as his grandfather had a generator installed in one of the outbuildings. Mains electricity only came to Bullwood in the early 1930s.

One thing that Stuart disliked very much was when the Admiralty or the Army Coastal Defence Authorities tested the coastal battery at the Fort at Ardhallow. "From Avondale," he recalled, "we could just see part of the conglomeration of the Fort with its flagstaff. When the flag was hoisted it was the signal that firing was about to take place. All householders in the area were notified beforehand to open windows, because the concussion from the firing guns could cause quite a lot of damage, even sometimes bringing down a ceiling, if care wasn't taken. An ominous looking little black tug would appear on the water towing three targets at hundred-yard intervals. The tug would sail directly in front of Avondale and there would be a shattering boom from the gun, the whine of a shell, and a huge plume of water when the shell struck the water. It always frightened me."

Stuart Peck recalled that in the 1920s and 1930s the bus service between Innellan and Dunoon was provided by McDiarmids of Innellan. McDiarmid, who was a man of great dignity, was generally accepted as 'The Provost of Innellan'. Two McDiarmid brothers, Tom and Alec, and Jock McGilp, drove the buses which were originally Ford model T charabancs. "Old Mr McDiarmid and his daughter used to take it in turns to sit in a little recess in the high wall directly opposite Innellan pier where Tom, Alec and Jock had to hand over the takings at the completion of each run. On Sundays, McDiarmid's bus would stop at the garden gate of Avondale, sound the horn and wait patiently to see if anyone wanted to go to church.

"In between Garail and Avondale was Garail Cottage where the Mackenzie family stayed. Old Faddy would sit on the porch with a very large telescope. He liked to watch the shipping going up and down the Clyde, but he was also very useful to the younger members of the family because he could train his telescope on the point, half-a-mile towards Innellan, and keep his eyes open for McDiarmid's bus coming along towards Dunoon. If anyone wanted to go shopping they would ask Faddy to give them a shout when he saw the bus, and then they would saunter down to the road in plenty of time to catch it.

"John McDiarmid's mauve buses had some opposition from two other operators – Proctor and Brown, with brown buses, and Antonelli's slightly grander blue tour buses.

"Sandy McKenzie had a yacht called *Para Handy* (shades of Neil Munro) moored off the cottage. One day during a September gale she started to drag her mooring. Sandy and two other men managed to launch the dinghy and went out to rig some sort of jib on her to keep her off the shore. But slowly and inexorably she blew towards the lee of Dunoon pier. Sandy managed to grab the iron ladder at the side of the pier and climbed up to be met by the piermaster who demanded pier dues!

"Near Avondale lived the Captain of an Anchor-Donaldson ship whose wife Maisie would get out her bed sheet whenever her husband came home. She would go down to the shore and wave it vigorously as the ship passed by. Although the big ships kept well over to the Renfrew side between the Cumbraes and the Cloch Lighthouse, the captain could obviously see the white sheet, because he would respond by blowing the ship's siren."

In 1936 Stuart Peck's grandmother died and Avondale had to be sold. The house was bought by ex-Provost Ferguson, and the traditional Provost's lamp-post was mounted over the archway of the front gate of the house, remaining there until some time after the Second World War.

23

Memories are Made of This

EVERYONE HAS A story to tell about the weather – be it good, bad or indifferent. Some will remember terrible storms and gale force winds, others flooding and ceaseless rain, whilst some recall droughts and the wells running dry. Yet, in reality, due to the currents of the Gulf Stream, the climate of Cowal is relatively douce and gentle without great extremes. In any case, it must be fairly healthy as there seem to be more centenarians in the West of Scotland than in many other parts of the country. Every few weeks or so there is a celebration of yet another person who has reached that marvellous age, which must be of great encouragement to anyone who longs for sunnier and warmer climes.

James Grieve, mentioned earlier in the book, seems to have been the oldest living man in the area. He died at the astonishing age of one hundred and eleven. Dying two years younger was Mrs Whyte, a widow who lived up Glen Lean. One day the minister came to pay his respects and, during a lull in the conversation, asked her how old she was. At that time Mrs Whyte was only one hundred and two and bitterly resented a man asking her age – her being a widow and all!

Mrs Chisholm, from Gourock, lived in Dunoon for many years and died in her one-hundred-and-eighth year as did Miss Violet Oswald, daughter of Dunoon's Provost in 1878, Archibald Oswald. Violet was the only person to have lived through Dunoon's century as a Burgh. In Dunoon churchyard is buried Archibald McArthur, who died in 1881, aged one hundred and four.

I was lucky to know Katherine Smith – Kate to all her friends – who lived to be just over one hundred and two. Mrs Smith, as I always called her, was a marvellous and spirited old lady with definite views on life, even when she was over a hundred. Although almost blind and fairly immobile, she kept up an interest in all that was going on and could, on occasion, become quite heated, particularly when politics and politicians were the issue. Kate Smith celebrated her one-hundredth birthday at a small party given for her and got up to make a splendid little impromptu 'thank you' speech – an achievement for anyone.

One of Dunoon's more remarkable characters was a man called Ernest G. Hartley, generally known as E.G. Robert Shiach recalled, "In the early 1900s E.G. was in Dunoon on holiday from his native Yorkshire when he heard that St John's Church was looking for an organist. He made enquiries at the manse, and was told that a short-list had been drawn up and those selected were to be playing that very afternoon. He turned up at the church at the appointed hour and asked the Session permission to sit in and hear the candidates playing. The four candidates were heard, and played very well. When they were finished, E.G. went to the front of the church where the Session were seated, explained that he was a visitor but that he would like to apply for the vacancy of organist. The Session were somewhat taken aback by this request and told him that they had decided to appoint one of the four applicants who had just finished playing. Hartley registered his disappointment but asked if they would mind if he tried out their fine organ. Rather reluctantly the request was granted and he played the Hallelujah Chorus. E.G. Hartley got the job! And for forty years he was the church's organist and choirmaster. His brother Harold was organist and choirmaster of the High Kirk and his son Leo became organist at St Cuthbert's. So the Hartleys were musically well represented in town."

David Brechin, too, had memories of the family and he recounted that E.G.'s enthusiasm was such that he carried his love of music into the naming of his children. "The eldest was Doris Olive who started the tonic solfa, Doh. His other children were Raymond, Ray; Monica, Me; Florence Adelaide, Fah; Stanley Oliver, Soh; Leo Angus, La. The only one who did not fit the tonic solfa scale was their youngest daughter Margery.

"When Mrs Hartley was expecting Stanley, a neighbour asked her, 'What will you call this one!' Mrs Hartley replied, 'My husband says Stanley Oliver if it's a boy or Sarah Olivia, if it's a girl.' 'Have a care Mrs Hartley,' warned the neighbour, 'the old man's having you on. He's taking you right up the scale!' "

The Hartley family lived at the appropriately named St Cecilia's, Victoria Road. Doris, the eldest daughter, taught Robert Shiach at the Grammar School where she was singing teacher between 1915 and 1918.

Robert recollected, "E.G. Hartley was a man of great enterprise. His main business at first was a music shop in Argyll Street, where Steven Gibson is now. There he sold sheet music, pianos and other musical instruments. In about 1912 he started up a motor-coach hiring business. His first two coaches were called *The Silver King* and *The Silver*

Queen. I remember E.G. telling me about one of the earlier ventures which was with a steam-driven coach. The trip started at Dunoon and the first stop was at Ardnadam Hotel where the passengers were invited to dismount and have a refreshment while E.G. stoked up the boiler for a good head of steam for the next stage.

"Argyll Hotel, near Robertson's Boatyard, was the next stop for another refreshment and stoke up, with the same routine at Cot House Hotel. Then the Coylet Hotel followed by Whistlefield Inn, where everyone had luncheon. That longer break was a real blessing for E.G. as it enabled him to get up enough steam for the climb up to the top of the hill, before the descent to Ardentinny. That, too, posed a bit of a problem as the coach had to be prevented from going downhill too fast. But Hartley was a man of great resource. He invited his passengers at the top of the hill to get out and view Loch Long. Then they held drag-ropes which E.G. had fitted to the hubs of the two rear wheels, thus providing a bit of brake power. Once on flat ground the passengers got back into the coach to refresh themselves at Ardentinny Hotel. This pantomime was repeated more or less on the return journey, and by the time the coach arrived back in Dunoon some of the passengers were not exactly sure where they had been, but as E.G. expressed it, 'They all had a lovely time.'

"E.G. Hartley was the first man in the country to run a 'Mystery Tour'. This usually took place in the evening, and after paying the fare of two shillings you were taken for a round-trip lasting two or three hours with no idea of your route or destination. Eventually E.G. increased the number of coaches and his fleet was called *The Silver Line* ."

There were many local characters and 'Abbie' MacDougall was one of them. Known to everyone as 'Abbie the Cabbie' he first drove a horse and carriage and, later on, a taxi. He was also a world-renowned breeder and exhibitor of show pigeons and sold prize pigeons all over the globe including the United States where his daughter, Gladys MacDonald, made her home. He was such a personality that the *Dunoon Observer* used to run a little comic-strip about him. 'Abbie' once got into trouble with the law because he had his precious pigeons in the cab with him while plying for hire. This must have been towards the end of the Second World War as Donald Macdonald remembered 'Abbie' writing an indignant letter to the *Dunoon Observer* in which he said something to the effect, 'Do not Churchill, Roosevelt and all the other bigwigs have their animals with them?'

In July 1945 'Abbie' stood for the local elections. At Castle Rocks he hoisted a large Union Jack beside the box on which he stood to address the crowd. The roadway was thronged with people to listen to him, and three months later he held a meeting at the Pavilion which he filled to capacity, several hundred people having to be turned away.

**Taking a break at Whistlefield Inn
before E. G. Hartley's steam coach
tours started in 1912**

But he lost the election to sixty-eight-year-old Mrs Helen Crawfurd Anderson, the first woman to become a Councillor in Dunoon.

Helen Anderson was born on 9th November 1877 in the Gorbals district of Glasgow, daughter of a master baker. The family moved to England when she was a child, and in her teens she returned to her native city. She was shocked by the Glasgow of the 1890s and this was the beginning of her deep involvement in helping the poor and under-privileged.

In 1898 she married the Reverend Alexander Montgomerie Crawfurd, whose church was situated in Glasgow's dockland. There, Helen heard the socialist politicians at their open-air meetings and, inspired by them, joined the suffragette movement. She was sent to prison three times for her political agitation and appeared in the dock with William Gallacher and other socialist leaders.

In 1921 she joined the newly formed Communist Party of Great Britain and when she was seventy-five chaired a session of the Scottish Congress of the Party.

Helen Crawfurd Anderson was a witty, distinguished-looking woman of warm personal charm with a single-minded devotion to the cause of the working class and the impoverished. Her fearlessness and courage made her respected and admired by friend and foe alike.

Helen died on 18th April 1954 aged seventy-seven. Her lifelong friend and associate, William Gallacher, gave a moving oration at her funeral and said, "Helen was so beautiful, in her mind and in her soul . . . there is so much I might say of her and yet fall far short of all she accomplished or all she sought to do."

Donald Macdonald remembered in the 1950s meeting William Gallacher, who was the first and last Communist Member of Parliament, at the house of Olindo Porchetta. Donald recollected that Olindo was very 'Scots' in sentiment. "He was by way of being a poet as well as an emphatic communist. He wrote two books to extol the Russian war effort during World War Two – *Hail My Red Muse* and *Heroes of the Vigil*."

Donald had memories of a rather less prestigious character, 'Happy Harry', whose supreme accolade uttered with some pride by his father-in-law was, "Harry wiz very popular in the jile." Donald recalled, "Happy Harry Wilson was so called because of his joyous religious conversion and he, too, may have been the archetype of the old Salvation Army story, 'Ah'm that happy ah could pit mah fit through the bloody big drom!' He was so well-known in the town, along with a porter at the pier and 'Abbie' MacDougall, that he, too, featured in a comic strip.

Dr Tom Fletcher was a friend of Mrs P. Rhodes who on her visits to his home in Dunoon, was always shown the most wonderful complete working model of a steam-engine or a magnificent model of a sailing ship. Tom was a medical practitioner but also a brilliant engineer and his hobby was making models. After his death, his model steam-engine was presented to the City of Bradford where it now has pride of place at the entrance area of the Cartwright Hall Museum, Lister Park, formerly the home of the Lister Family.

Tom Fletcher was also a very clever horologist and the Rhodes family used to spend hours watching him in his workroom making minute parts for use in clock repairs. He undertook to repair the local church clock in Dunoon and successfully got it working and striking again after a major breakdown. Tom took great pride in keeping a watchful eye on it – no mean feat climbing the tower for a man over seventy.

Dunoon has had its fair share of men connected with the sea. David Beveridge, a retired master mariner who lived in Sydney, Australia, said, "After thirty years of seafaring the most beautiful approach to Britain, especially after a long voyage in 'furrin pairts' was that past Dunoon. We ex-mariners had a saying, 'When Ailsa Craig ye see ahead, pack your bag and dump your bed.' That, of course, was in the days when you didn't have all the wonderful amenities which prevail today."

David lived most of his life in Dunoon before emigrating and remembered well John MacVicar who gave himself the honorary title of 'Captain'. "One summer's day, in the height of the season, a visitor wanted to hire a rowing-boat from Captain MacVicar. The old shellback was very reluctant to entrust his boat with its gleaming, sparkling coat of varnish to a 'Glesca' keelie' who probably didn't know a rowlock from a spinnaker. Captain Mac, hummed and haawed, and looking at the darkening sky said, 'No, laddie, I dinna think so. There is a big swell coming up from the south.' 'Aw,' said the Glaswegian, 'Is ma money no as guid as his?' "

The great-great-great-grandparents, Captain James and Margaret Macfie, of Swedish Ulf Macfie Hagman, spent most of their life in Dunoon. In 1807, Captain James was sailing his ship, the brigantine *Garland*, for Buenos Aires. The ship was fairly near port when she disappeared in a gale. Margaret (who was also born a Macfie) lived at the time at Gairhallow Lodge, and never put on the customary black clothes as she would not admit that her husband was drowned. The poor woman – every day she expected James to arrive home.

G. R. Stewart had an uncle, James Stewart, living in Dunoon in the 1920s, who was a well-known personality in the town. James lived at Hillcrest, Alexander Street, where he came to retire after fifty-two years in the Merchant Navy.

James had gone to sea at the age of fourteen, serving his apprenticeship with the Loch Line and gaining an extra master's certificate at the age of twenty-five. He also served with the Anchor Line and ships under foreign flags.

While second officer of the SS *Larnaca* in 1895, he assisted in the rescue of ten men of the *Alfred* in a gale. On this occasion he sustained a broken collar-bone but carried on. For this bravery he was decorated by the Liverpool Shipwreck and Humane Society. Captain Stewart was also decorated by the Norwegian Government during the First World War when he rescued a Norwegian sailor by diving from his own ship into a stormy Atlantic ocean.

Another interesting relative of G. R. Stewart was his Aunt Peggy who lived at Struan, Mary Street. When she was young she had a most unusual job. As she had perfect copperplate handwriting she was employed, before the days of typewriters, in the big Glasgow warehouse R. W. Forsyth.

A seafaring man from Dunoon was Marion Corkhill's grandfather, Captain David Leslie, who was quite a 'man o' parts'. Captain Leslie took part in the American Civil War as a blockade-runner, carrying ammunition for the Confederates. On the return journeys he would bring back cotton for the Lancashire cotton mills, where the people were starving for want of work. This trade was not officially backed by the Government, but they turned a blind eye for the sake of the ailing cotton industry.

David was captured three times during the war and escaped twice, the war ending soon after his third arrest, which was during the 'run' in the famous *Banshee.*

Leslie's career at sea ended soon after when he offered his ship and services to the Italian patriot Garibaldi who was looking for a vessel to transport his 'thousand' redshirts to Italy to help in the Italian War of Independence. Garibaldi presented Leslie with a handsome gold ring in recognition of his services. He also gave him one of his famous red shirts.

David Leslie then retired to Dunoon and built Bermuda Villa where Marion Corkhill was born. Cemented down in front of the steps leading to the door of the house are white pebbles in which is inserted, in black pebbles, the word *Banshee.* On his retirement Leslie was made a Police Commissioner and one of his jobs was to enquire into the morals and lives of people wishing to settle in Dunoon!

The Revd Dr William Neil's grandmother owned a house in Dunoon, and as a child he spent all his holidays in the town. His widow, Effie Lindsay, recalled that when he was quite a small lad he fell off Dunoon pier and was rescued by a man who jumped into the water to save him. That unknown rescuer certainly saved a boy who was to become widely known in later years for his numerous writings, both scholarly and popular, on the Bible, and for his distinguished broadcasts on religious topics.

William Neil was born on 13th July 1909 and went to school and university in Glasgow. After continuing his studies at Heidelberg, Germany, William returned to Glasgow as assistant to the Professor of Biblical Criticism.

During the Second World War William Neil was an army chaplain and was mentioned several times in dispatches. Neil's most cherished honour was the honorary D.D. awarded him by his Alma Mater.

Another clergyman, the Rev W. D. Laird, also came from Dunoon where his father, James, had a grocer's shop in Hillfoot Street. James was a member of the old Parish Council and of his Ward Committee, as well as being active in the Freemasons as Right Worshipful Master of his Lodge. Being a licensed grocer he felt reluctant to become an Elder in the Parish Church to which he belonged, but was eventually persuaded.

The Rev Laird reminisced, "At one time in the Lodge there was an unusual situation, my father, the licensed grocer, was the Lodge chaplain and I, the theological student, was the Lodge piper!"

R. K. Arthur had memories of a grocer's shop, but obviously it was not the one belonging to James Laird. "I will not reveal the then well-known name, probably now forgotten, which in peeling paint was emblazoned over the narrow doorway. Narrow, because it was perpetually flanked with barrels of oatmeal (with wooden lid), apples, sacks of potatoes and other miscellany. I remember when the oatmeal lid was lifted seeing a couple of contented mice leisurely walking away!

"The proprietor seemed ancient (about my own present age of seventy-five) as he fumbled around, handicapped by bottle-lensed metal specs on the end of his nose which occasionally fell into the meal- or flour-bin. The grocer never stood still, even when the shop was empty, immediately alert at the sign of a customer, his restless hands needlessly arranging everything within reach. When he spoke he lisped badly, spluttering saliva over everything within a yard which made me cringe when buying bacon or butter, and he kept on and on patting the latter between his hands, sometimes muddy after weighing potatoes or turnips.

"When sent for the messages I had quite a long run to the shops, and my mother was not aware that I usually went to this particular grocer, being the nearest shop by half a mile. When I heard her, with amused horror, describe the grocer's antics, I smiled to myself and thought, 'What the eyes don't see, the heart doesn't grieve over.' "

R. K. Arthur's father was quite a character. He was obsessed with sailing and swimming and was the first man in Dunoon to have red sails on his 14-foot lugger. He made R.K. perform a summer chore that the boy hated. About the middle of May, the local paper would announce that summer had commenced as Mr 'X' had started diving off his own boat. R.K. recalled, "I had to meet this man every day at 4pm prompt at Cargill's boat stance and give him dry towels. In mid-September the paper would announce summer at an end as Mr 'X' had stopped diving. What a relief!"

Another character that stuck in the memory of R. K. Arthur was Jimmy Andrews. Jimmy lived alone in a tiny cottage in Hillfoot Street. R.K. recalled, "Jimmy was a kenspeckle figure in Dunoon and a great antagonist of my father, because he was slightly better at sailing, and consequently there was a permanent animosity. He kept a great bale of rosy-brown Harris Tweed and just replaced his plus-fours as necessary. His only other garment was a perfect evening suit, for he attended all the local functions and dances where he usually got mildly drunk.

"He made an annual pilgrimage to Oban Regatta in his beautiful little lugsail boat and returned in September to lay up his boat for the winter. One winter he failed to return and it was assumed that he had foundered. However, come March, his little white sail appeared again. Evidently, on leaving Oban in September, Jimmy had turned right instead of left, finishing up in Stornoway where he got himself some cosy digs and remained for the rest of the winter."

Dunoon had many interesting piermasters, one of whom was Captain Dugald Cameron, whose nephew, Commander Donald Cameron, received a V.C. for his part in the attack on the *Tirpitz* in 1942 in the fjords of Norway. His courageous exploit was the subject of a film starring John Mills called *Above Us The Waves*, for which Commander Cameron was appointed technical adviser. Dugald Cameron died in 1940 and there were eighty applications for his job!

Paul Hutton remembered after the Second World War piermaster William Beattie. "We boys used to call him Admiral Beattie and he had a hard time trying to keep us off his cross-beams under the pier. It was by far the best place for catching flounders as it had a nice flat sandy bottom. Although it was undoubtedly dangerous, it was an adventure and a challenge, even at the risk of falling in, or worse, being caught and having your backside dusted by Admiral Beattie and then by one's own father." Paul looked back on his childhood in Dunoon with a great deal of affection. "Dunoon had really everything that a boy could wish for – the sea, the shore, the old slate mine that sometimes even produced 'fool's gold', and that enchanted 'Tarzan's Jungle' – Morag's Fairy Glen. Dunoon is a place such as I have yearned for in many other lands, but have never found."

Dunoon may have changed since Paul Hutton was a lad and yet for many people it still provides enchantment and pleasure. The town and its surrounding countryside and shoreside villages are still unspoilt: no unsightly high-rise buildings mar Cowal's scenic beauty. Long may it remain so.

Bibliography

Argyll and Bute Nigel Tranter

Argyll and the Souther n Hebrides David Graham Campbell

Argyllshire and Buteshir e Peter MacNair

Benn – Blue Guide to Scotland Edited L. Russell Muirhead

Black Maria, The, or The Criminals' Omnibus Edited Harry Hodge

Black's Guide to Glasgow and its Envir ons

Britannia and Her Contemporaries B Heckstall Smith

British Music Hall Roy Busby

British Yachts and Yachtsmen

Caledonian Steam Packet Co. Ltd, The Iain C MacArthur

Campbells of Kilmun, The Iain Hope

Chambers Biographical Dictionary

Clyde, The Neil Munro

Clyde Passenger Steamers – 1812-1901, The Captain James Williamson

Clyde Piers Ian McCrorie and Joy Monteith

Coasts of Dunoon and Clyde George Eyre Todd

Colegate's Guide to Dunoon, Hunter's Quay and Kir n

Collins Encyclopedia of Scotland Edited John Keay & Julia Keay

Cooper's Creek Alan Morehead

Cowal Chronicle, The Humphrey J. Dingley

Cruise in Company George Blake and Christopher Small

Days at the Coast Hugh MacDonald

Dictionary of National Biography

Dictionary of V ictorian Painters Christopher Wood

Drove Roads of Scotland, The A.R.B. Haldane

Dunoon in the 1820s Major A.J.M. Bennett

Dunoon 1868-1968 Jack House

Dunoon and the Coasts of Clyde George Eyre Todd

Dunoon Herald

Dunoon of Old, The Angus McLean

Dunoon Observer and Ar gyllshire Standard

Dunoon Of ficial Guide Jack House

Education in Ar gyll 1872-1972 Donald MacKechnie & James H Tyre

Educational History of Dunoon and Kilmun   Thomas A. Small
Elizabeth Gaskell, Mrs Winifred Gérin
Encyclopaedia Britannica
England in the Late Middle Ages – 1307-1536 A. E. Myers
England in the Seventeenth Century Ashley Maurice
Everyman's Dictionary of Literary Biography Edited D.C. Browning
Everyman's Factfinder
Fifty years of Railway Life in England, Scotland and Ireland
                                                        Joseph Tatlow
Firth of Clyde, The W.D. Cocker
Forestry Commission Guide
Further Memories Robert Louis Stevenson
Glasgow Cowal Society
          Speech by Lt.Col. William Rose Campbell of Ballochyle
Glasgow Encyclopedia Joe Fisher
Glasgow's Herald Alastair Phillips
Glasgow Past and Present Senex, Alquis etc.
Glasgow's Treasure Chest James Cowan
Gleanings Sir Norman Lamont
Glory of Scotland, The J.J. Bell
Great Yachts Philip McCutchan
Guinness Book of Theatre, The Michael Billington
Herald, The
Highways and Byways in the West Highlands Seton Gordon
History of Argyll, The Colin M. MacDonald
History of the Clan Lamont Sir Norman Lamont
History of Cowal, The Archibald Brown
History of Cowal Highland Gathering, A William Laidlaw Inglis
History of the English Speaking Peoples Winston S. Churchill
History of Langbank Bridget Mackenzie
Ingenious Mr Bell, The Brian D. Osborne
Inglis's Guide to Dunoon
Innellan Rev. John C. Hill
International Film Encyclopaedia, The Ephraim Katz
Jessie McLachlan William Roughead
Johnston's Guide to Dunoon
Kilmun Arboretum and Forest Plots
King's Grocer, The Bob Crampsey
Leaves from the Lipton Logs Sir Thomas J. Lipton, Bt.
Life of George Matheson, The D Macmillan
Listener, The
Liverpool Echo
MacBrayne's Summer Tours of the Highlands
Murray's Handbooks for Scotland – The Clyde

Music Review, The
National Commercial Directory
            of the Whole of Scotland and the Isle of Man
New Hutchinson Twentieth Century Encyclopaedia, The
Notes on Dunoon and Neighbour hood Thomas Dunlop
Official Guide to Dunoon George Eyre Todd
Official Guide – Dunoon and the Coast of the Clyde
Our History Margaret T. Johnstone
Oxford Companion to Ships and the Sea, The Edited Peter Kemp
Oxford Companion to Sports and Games, The Edited John Arlott
Pelican History of England, The
Prominent Pr ofiles J. M Hamilton
Readers' Encyclopaedia, The William Rose Benét
Records and Recollections Augusta Lamont
River Runs to W ar, A John D. Drummond
'Roamin in the Gloamin' Sir Harry Lauder
Round and About Dunoon Nancy Stirling
Sceptre Hugh Somerville
Scots, The Clifford Hanley
Scots Magazine, The
Scottish Historical Review
Scottish Portrait Augustus Muir
Scottish W estern Holiday Haunts T. C. F. Brotchie
Sketch of Explorations John McKinlay
Souvenir Pr ogramme – Civic W eek – Diamond Jubilee 1868-1928
Statistical Account of Scotland Sir John Sinclair Bt.
Tartan Pimper nel, The Donald C. Caskie
Through the Glens of Cowal Nancy Stirling
Times, The
Todd's Guide to Dunoon
Tourists' Guide to Dunoon, Innellan etc.
Tourists Guides Thr oughout the Decades
Tudor England S. T. Bindoff
Two Centuries of Education in Dunoon John MacGregor
West of Scotland V isitor
When I Was A Boy General Sir Ian Hamilton

Index

Sheep and cattle used to be transported to markets on the steamers before regulations required that they were put on closed vehicles. The animals would be penned on the deck and when discharged, decks would be cleaned and hosed down

Before the days of the steamers, drovers from the Isles and the north would bring their cattle to Dunoon for the short crossing to Cloch Point. Villagers would complain at the regular influx of animals grazing the land, sometimes for days on end if conditions were unfavourable for the crossing

COWAL
Hospice
TRUST
FOR THOSE WHO CARE

Cowal Hospice Trust was established to raise funds to provide a hospice facility to serve Dunoon and the Cowal area of Argyllshire.

The aim of the hospice movement is to provide a high quality palliative care service for the terminally ill, as well as a comprehensive support system for their families, carers and friends. A hospice provides services which tend not to be available from other sources.

The Cowal Hospice Trust has entered into a partnership with the Argyll & Bute NHS Trust to create a two- to four- bedded facility within Dunoon and District General Hospital, but having its own identity and entrance.

All royalties from the sale of *Memories of Dunoon & Cowal* will be donated to the Cowal Hospice Trust.